Start with a Story

LITERATURE AND LEARNING
IN YOUR CLASSROOM

Linda Wason-Ellam

HEINEMANN
Portsmouth, NH

Authorship is not a solitary task. I would like to thank my supportive cast: Dr. Benjamin John Ellam, my husband, who has been the Wind Beneath My Wings; Courtney Wason Bardonner, my daughter, for her editorial assistance; Jean Hoeft, language arts consultant; Anne Davis, teacher, Calgary Board of Education, and Sharon Huebner, Rockyview School Division, Calgary, for their suggestions; my editor, David Kilgour, for helping me shape the manuscript; education students at the University of Saskatchewan who shared so generously; and, of course, the children everywhere who keep us challenged.

© 1991 Pembroke Publishers Limited
  528 Hood Road
  Markham, Ontario
  L3R 3K9

Published in the U.S.A. by
Heinemann Educational Books, Inc.
361 Hanover Street
Portsmouth, NH 03801-3959
ISBN (U.S.) 0-435-08591-3

Canadian Cataloguing in Publication Data

Wason-Ellam, Linda, 1942–
  Start with a story

Includes bibliographical references.
ISBN 0-921217-62-5

1. Literature – Study and teaching (Elementary).
2. Language arts (Elementary). 3. Reading
(Elementary) – Language experience approach.
4. Children – Books and reading. I. Title.

LB1575.W38   372.64′044   C91-093368-5

Library of Congress Cataloging-in-Publication Data

Wason-Ellam, Linda, 1942-
  Start with a story: literature and learning in your classroom/
Linda Wason-Ellam.
        p.   cm.
  Includes bibliographical references.
  ISBN 0-435-08591-3

  1. Literature – Study and teaching (Elementary) – Canada.
2. Language arts (Elementary) – Canada. 3. Reading (Elementary) – Canada –
Language experience approach. 4. Children – Canada – Books
and reading. 5. Education, Elementary – Canada – Activity programs.
I. Title.

LB1575.5.C2W37 1991   91-11268
372.6′044′0971 – dc20   CIP

Editor: David Kilgour
Design: John Zehethofer
Cover Illustration: Rossitza Scortcheva
Typesetting: Jay Tee Graphics Ltd.

Printed and bound in Canada
9 8 7 6 5 4 3 2

Contents

Introduction

This book is intended to help teachers who are trying to implement a "whole language" approach to using literature in their classrooms. The theory that children will learn more effectively and happily by reading stories and creating their own in a positive, child-centred environment has taken hold in schools across the continent. Unfortunately, however, making the theory a reality can require a lot of work for teachers who are already burdened with crushing workloads. My goal is to lighten the burden by outlining strategies and activities that can be used by any elementary school teacher who wants to integrate literature into the classroom.

The glue that holds this book together is the incredible treasure trove of stories and books available to us as teachers. Hundreds are listed here, both in the text and in bibliographies at the end of the book, with suggested activities ranging from simple — reading a story to students — to fairly complex — mounting a play based on a story. All the activities revolve around stories and books of many kinds, from wordless picture books to poetry, from novels to non-fiction. And the activities range from reading and writing to often overlooked but nonetheless vital ones such as listening and talking, viewing, art, music, and drama, all of which can enrich childrens' experience of literature. I have kept theory to a minimum, and outlined each activity briefly. This is partly so that you can adapt these ideas to your own style and needs, but also because I have covered a lot of territory: whole books have been written, for instance, about drama alone. My book is a sort of introductory survey to the possible uses of literature in schools. For more specific applications in particular areas of the curriculum, you may want to consult more specialized professional books.

To identify students of different skill levels, I have used the terms "beginning" readers, by which I mean children who have little or no experience with reading or literature, and "developing" readers, who have progressed enough to read or write on their own with some fluency. The terms are deliberately vague: only you can determine what sorts of story experiences your students want and can handle. My hope is that you will find literature here that you can use in all areas of your curriculum, and for whatever purpose your needs — and those of your students — require.

CHAPTER ONE

Listening and Talking

Why Teach Listening and Talking?

Most teachers now recognize that language learning is an active process. Students must hear language used and have many opportunities to use it themselves in order to grow linguistically. Whole language classrooms are places where students can view, listen, talk, read, and write, where they have the chance to initiate, listen to, and use language for their own purposes in a variety of settings.

Students must develop a fluent oral language base before they learn to read and write, and yet the skills involved in talking and listening are taught rarely, if at all. Nonetheless, students naturally use talk all the time, for informal activities such as conversations, sharing opinions, and solving problems, and for formal activities including interviewing, storytelling, role-playing, and reporting. Many of these talk activities are integrated into the entire curriculum.

Listening can be defined as the interpretation of a message. Listeners make meaning by assimilating, accommodating, and integrating messages. We all use listening for a variety of purposes. Listening can be appreciative (i.e., for enjoyment), comprehensive (to understand a message), critical (to evaluate a message), and empathetic (to understand others). As with talking, listening is part of every classroom — and often not taught at all.

The activities described in this chapter are designed for instruction rather than for practice (students will practise talking and listening constantly on their own). They will help students attend to important information in messages and to communicate ideas clearly and concisely, a skill which is necessary for participation in many of the literary activities we will encounter later.

Personal Sharing and Responding

Personal sharing and responding activities provide practice in communicating effectively. Personal sharing can take several forms depending on the oral language skills of the students and the grade level.

Group Sharing

Sharing Time or Meeting Time: This should be done informally, allowing students to speak in their own, unrehearsed words. Each speaker shares information or a story and learns that he or she must have something interesting to say in order to get the attention of the group. The listener responds by adding ideas or asking relevant questions. This activity works better when the class is divided into smaller groups of five or six, as this allows more students to participate.

Magic Circle: Magic circle is an interactive activity which provides an opportunity to deal with values and feelings using spontaneous language. Students sit in a circle with only one requirement: when the speaker shares and describes a value or a personal feeling, everyone must listen. The listeners can respond to the speaker and reflect on that value or feeling. This encourages speakers and listeners to be more sensitive to each other.

Oral Reporting: Oral reporting is a more formal activity involving planned language. The speaker must study and prepare background material. The listener can respond to the speaker's ideas by expanding and challenging the ideas or asking relevant questions.

Partner Sharing

Personal Storytelling: Students work in pairs. Each student takes a turn at being a speaker while the other is listener. The speaker tells the other person a true story about something that is of personal importance. The listener's role is to listen attentively and not interrupt except to ask questions and encourage the speaker. After the speaker has finished, the listener repeats the story as accurately as possible. Afterwards students switch roles.

Echo Dialogue: Each student practises listening to what someone is saying by echoing the other person in a conversation. Every time one talks to the other, the listener must first repeat what was said before replying. The speaker must agree that the paraphrase is accurate before continuing.

Comprehensive Listening and Responding

Comprehensive listening and responding activities help teach and facilitate students' comprehension.

Oral Cloze

An oral cloze technique can be used to help students focus on making meaning while listening to a repetitive story. While you read or tell the story, pause at the end of a sentence and wait for the students to supply the predictable word. Oral cloze activities train listeners to use semantic and syntactic clues: based on "what makes sense" in the story and their own experience, the students can fill in the missing word quite easily.

Encourage listening for meaning by sharing Nicki Weiss's *An Egg Is an Egg*, stopping at the last word in each stanza and inviting predictions:

An egg is an egg,
Until it hatches.
Then it is a   __.

Students can respond with a number of possibilities that make syntactic and semantic sense:

> *chick*
> *bird*
> *snake*
> *turtle*
> *ostrich*

A longer selection might be Rose Bonne's *I Know an Old Lady:*

I know an old lady who swallowed a cat.
Now fancy that, to swallow a cat!
She swallowed a cat to catch a _____.

Stories with repeated phrases or repetitive sentence patterns are the easiest to use as a beginning activity.

For Beginning Listeners: The repetitive patterns in A.G. Deming's *Who Is Tapping at My Window?*, Janina Domanska's *Busy Monday Morning*, Nicki Weiss's *Dog Boy Cap Skate*, or Jane O'Connor's *The Teeny Tiny Woman* work well for oral cloze and invite predictions.

For Developing Listeners: Try using rhyming poetry with older students. Share the clever poems of Lois Simmie in *Auntie's Knitting a Baby* and *An Armadillo Is Not a Pillow* or Patricia Polacco's contemporary version of Ernest Lawrence Thayer's *Casey at the Bat: A Ballad of the Republic, Sung in the Year 1888.*

Anticipating Future Action or Events of a Story

Predicting actions or events in a story helps listeners actively make inferences and integrate them, a critical thinking process that is similar to those used by readers and writers as they focus on making meaning. Choose a high-interest short story to read to the group. If the students listen attentively, they will anticipate the action or events of the story as you read. Whenever you come to a critical point, stop reading and ask the students what will happen next. **Caution:** the intention is never to guess the "right answer" but to consider plausible alternatives justified by clues in the story. Stop at the climax of the story and discuss alternative endings. Finally, finish the original story and ask the students which ending they preferred and why.

Stories with lots of action naturally lend themselves to predicting events and actions.

For Beginning Listeners: Share Barbara Shook Hazen's *Tight Times*, Mirra Ginsburg's *The Magic Stove*, or Steven Kellogg's *The Island of the Skog* by stopping at frequent intervals and asking, "What do you think might happen next?" An alternate choice would be Miriam Nerlove's rhyming couplets which invite listeners to guess "Mistakes Made" in *I Made a Mistake*.

One variation is to read a short story to students and pause before the final event in it. Ask students to predict what they think will happen in the concluding event and write their own version as a news report. After students write their endings, compare their predictions to the original story. Stories which have action and surprise endings, such as Edward Marshall's *Space Case* or Jane Johnson's *Today I Thought I'd Run Away*, are excellent for this activity.

Another variation is to ask the students to add a character to the story and decide how the insertion of this character might change it. Then have them rewrite the story in an alternate format (a dialogue, an interview, a feature story, a letter, etc.).

For Developing Listeners: More suspenseful story plots work well with older students. Jane Leslie Conly's *Rasco and the Rats of NIMH*, a sequel to her father's *Mrs. Frisby and the Rats of NIMH*, and Alfred Slote's beginning science fantasy, *The Trouble on Janus*, will challenge listeners to predict the plot based on clues in the story. A more challenging selection would be Margaret Laurence's time-shift fantasy, *The Olden Days Coat*.

Drawing Details from a Story

Visualizing and drawing story details help students make inferences about explicit and implicit information heard while listening. Story details can be the setting, the physical traits, or the actions of characters.

Ask students to listen carefully and try to visualize the setting or characters in a story. Be sure to read enough of the story to provide an understanding of character, setting, and plot. After reading, ask students to draw either the setting or a character in the passage. Display the drawings along with the printed passage.

This activity works well if you read junior fiction (without showing the students the illustrations), as the setting in most picture books is usually illustrated in the pictures rather than described in much detail.

For Beginning Listeners: Before sharing the pictures with students, read Diane Siebert's *Mojave* and Ruth Yaffe Radin's *A Winter Place*. Then ask them to draw the setting as described in the story.

For Developing Listeners: *Owls in the Family* by Farley Mowat is an excellent story to use. Read the first eight paragraphs of this story, which describe the details of springtime in Saskatoon, Saskatchewan.

Alternate suggestions are Paula Fox's loving depiction of a Greek island in *Lily and the Lost Boy*, or Byrd Baylor's rich verse about Grandpa's hometown in *The Best Town in the World*.

Sequencing Story Segments

Sequencing story segments encourages students to hypothesize the plot development of a story. Duplicate a short story that the students have not yet heard or read, such as Robert San Souci's *The Enchanted Tapestry*. Cut it up into various segments, then distribute the segments among several students. Prepare an uncut version in advance, lightly marking the places where the cut sections begin. Read the story, pausing when you come to a cut portion. The student who thinks he or she has the next segment of the story then reads it to the class. A longer selection might be Susan Cooper's *The Silver Cow*.

Literary Patterning

Patterned stories in which words and actions are repeated to carry the action forward are useful for choral speaking and listening activities. After listening to the story pattern, students can join in with their own predictions of what will happen in the story. *Over in the Meadow* by Olive Wadsworth works well as a pattern story.

Over in the meadow, in the sand, in the sun,
Lived an old mother turtle and her little turtle one. . . .

One variation is to have students improvise on the literary pattern by creating and taping their own versions:

Out in a galaxy on a planet near the sun,
Lived an old mother spaceship and her little spaceship one.
"Beep!", said the mother.
"I beep," said the one.
So he beeped all day,
On a planet near the sun.

Improvising Literary Dialogue

Many repetitive stories provide opportunities for participating and expanding the literary dialogue. In *You Look Ridiculous Said the Hippopotamus to the Rhinoceros* by Bernard Waber, a question and response pattern is repeated throughout and students can be invited to role-play story characters and predict their dialogue. In response to the question, "Do you think I look ridiculous?", a number of students can assume the roles of animal characters. They can respond by listening to each other and dialoguing the literary interaction.

Giraffe: "I think you look ridiculous because you do not have a long, long neck like mine."
Hippopotamus: "Why do I need a long, long neck like you?"
Giraffe: "You need a long, long neck, Hippopotamus, so you can reach those juicy leaves on the high branches."

Title/Headline Summaries

Listening for the main idea of a story or piece of non-fiction can be reinforced by summarizing it.

Read aloud a short story, a chapter from a junior novel, or a paragraph from an informational text. Then ask students to write a suitable title or headline for it. Help students realize the idea that the title or headline is a summary that contains the main idea.

For Beginning Listeners: Younger listeners can brainstorm many different story titles for a favorite literary selection. When reading Robert Munsch's *Jonathan Cleaned Up — Then He Heard a Sound, or Blackberry Subway Jam,* Pat Hutchins's *Don't Forget the Bacon,* or Alice and Martin Provensen's *The Glorious Flight across the Channel with Louis Blériot, July 25, 1909,* have students suggest some alternative or less complex story titles.

For Developing Listeners: Have older students summarize the main ideas of informational text after reading Seymour Simon's *Jupiter* and *Saturn,* two straightforward texts that are accompanied by full-color photographs that were transmitted by the unmanned Voyger spacecraft.

You can extend this activity — or others in this chapter — by tape-recording a chapter or a series of articles, then making it available at a Listening Centre so that students can work independently.

Brainstorming Story Problems

Brainstorming enables students to generate as many ideas as possible in response to a question. It helps activate prior knowledge as well as test new ideas. In brainstorming, all answers are acceptable, the goal being the quantity of ideas and the uncritical acceptance of them. "What if?" problems are good for brainstorming. Following the model of Mercer Mayer's *What Do You Do with a Kangaroo?* you might improvise on the text and add story characters. For instance, ask students, "What would you do if there was a boa constrictor on your bedpost?"

Students can practise divergent thinking by generating alternate solutions to the problems that story characters encounter in folk and fairy tales.

For Beginning Listeners: Discuss how the two quarreling cats can resolve their problem of dividing the spoils of the hunt in Yoshiko Uchida's *The Two Foolish Cats*, how Jack can make the sad princess laugh in *Lazy Jack*, or what other ways one clever animal can match wits with King Leopard in Ruby Dee's *Two Ways to Count to Ten: A Liberian Folktale*.

For Developing Listeners: Share George Shannon's *Stories to Solve: Folktales from Around the World*, a collection of story problems, or brainstorm other ways the resourceful little people can create a miniature world in N.M. Bodecker's *Quimble Wood*.

CHAPTER TWO

Viewing

There is no doubt that we live in a visual age. From infancy, children are exposed to images through television, films, videos, photographs, paintings, billboards, computer screens — and the list goes on. The power of all these images can be used very effectively to teach language skills by getting students to respond to what they see through talking, writing, dramatizing, or making art of their own.

Seeing is a physical process, but using what has been seen is a mental, or cognitive, process. As students view the world, they can assimilate new data into their knowledge and fine-tune their ability to handle the ideas of which words are symbols. For this reason, it is important to incorporate viewing experiences into all areas of the curriculum.

The principles of listening and talking described in the last chapter should be applied to viewing as much as to reading. Encouraging students to think about what they are seeing is a way to heighten their perceptions of the experience. Brainstorming together enables students to discover words and ultimately thoughts that might never have surfaced if students were view-

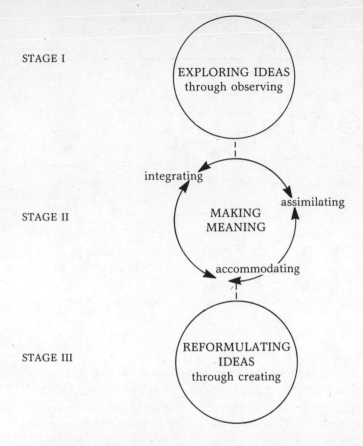

STAGE I — EXPLORING IDEAS through observing

STAGE II — MAKING MEANING (integrating, assimilating, accommodating)

STAGE III — REFORMULATING IDEAS through creating

ing and generating words on their own. Ideas and words spring forth as students respond to images in books, slides, or other media.

The diagram above illustrates how viewing can lead to learning.

Images in Books

The use of picture books in reading programs will be dealt with later, but it is worth noting that some of them lend themselves particularly well to enriching visual experience. Many picture books, for instance, encourage readers to find hidden objects in pictures or predict what is going to happen next. Illustrations in other books help students become aware of details or moods.

Some offer experiences in counting or classification. When these books are grouped together, students are able to compare one work with another, and these story experiences involve them in both cognitive development and language learning.

For Beginning Learners: Younger students enjoy picture puzzles and looking for hidden objects. Familiar story characters are hiding in the illustrations of Janet and Allen Ahlberg's *Each Peach Pear Plum*, wild animals are lurking in Ann Jonas's *The Trek*, jungle animals are watching in Pat Hutchins's counting book, *One Hunter*, animals are camouflaged in José Aruego and Ariane Dewey's *We Hide, You Seek*, and animals are a visual puzzle in Suse MacDonald and Bill Oakes's *Puzzlers*. Viewers can interact with books by guessing who causes a boat to sink in Pamela Allen's *Who Sank the Boat?*, identifying shapes in Pam Adams and Ceri Jones's *I Thought I Saw*, and matching animals to eyes in Jill Bailey's *Animals of Course! Eyes*. Viewers can match their perceptions with the three princesses as they disagree about the appearance of a tree in different seasons in Freya Littledale's *The Magic Plum Tree*.

Some books show students new ways to consider well-known materials, while others furnish new and different images, ideas, or perspectives. Ann Jonas's *Round Trip* shows a trip from a small town through the country to the city. When the book is turned upside down and read backwards, it tells the story of the trip back home. Seymour Chwast's *Tall City, Wide Country* can be read forward and backward: it is held vertically for the tall city and horizontally for the wide country. Similarly, the illustrations change as the reader's perspective is altered in Beau Gardner's *The Look Again . . . . and Again, and Again and Again Book* and Ruth Brown's *If at First You Do Not See*. Jan Adkins uses cutaway drawings in *Inside: Seeing beneath the Surface* to help students visualize and generalize about the insides of different objects. Ruth Heller shows how animals hide in her *How to Hide a Crocodile and Other Reptiles* and five other titles in this camouflage series.

Tina Hoban stretches young viewers' imaginations in the photographic texts *Is It Rough? Is It Smooth? Is It Shiny?*, *Round and Round and Round*, and *Take Another Look*, Joan Elma Rahn extends the understanding of concepts through photographs in *Holes*, and Peter Ziebel challenges the observation of familiar objects which are distorted in *Look Closer*. All these books can be used with groups or individuals, the teacher asking questions and encouraging students to discuss their own reactions to the images.

For Developing Learners: Mitsumasa Anno's wordless books help older children develop group observational skills. Give readers a list of historical and literary characters to look for in the full-page illustrations in *Anno's Journey, Anno's Italy,* or *Anno's Britain*. The details in Peter Cross's *Trouble for Trumpets* keep the viewer fascinated with imaginary experiences. Searching for black and white objects in Peter Catalanatto's wordless book, *Dylon's Day Out,* is both fun and revealing. Historical texts like Aliki's *A Medieval Feast* present informational details about life in medieval times. John Goodall's *The Story of an English Village* identifies the changes in a village through the centuries. Books such as Seymour Simon's *Jupiter* and *The Long View into Space*, and Melvin Zisfein's *Flight: A Panorama of Aviation*, are photographic essays that extend students' knowlege about explorations in space. Ron and Nancy Goor's *In the Driver's Seat* puts viewers behind the wheel in trucks, cars, jets, and tanks, while Gail Gibbons's illustrations in Joanna Cole's *Cars and How They Go* show the intricate mechanics of automobiles. There is an increasing number of non-fiction books lavishly illustrated and published in picture book format. These books can develop complex ideas through drawings, diagrams, or photographs that illustrate terminology and encourage students to interact with the text by observing and identifying.

The National Council of Teachers of English publishes a list of trade books, *Adventuring with Books*, edited by Mary Jett Simpson. This review provides teachers and librarians with information about locating recommended books that can be used for instruction in the classroom.

Slides

Photographic slides can be used to develop meaning and to provide background for language in the same way as pictures in books. If you have access to them, collect slides of clouds, rain, sunsets, trees, cities, countryside, bridges, etc. — whatever interests you and your students.

If you cannot make your own slides, commercially produced slides are available. Better still, use illustrations from literary selections such as Peter Parnall's *Winter Barn,* Ron Hirschi's *Who Lives on the Prairie?*, Joanne Ryder's *Step into the Night*, or Jeanne Titherington's *Where Are You Going Emma?* Many science and social studies books contain full-page photographs or elaborate illustrations.

Brainstorming Sensory Language

Ask your students to look at a slide of a scenic location and develop sensory language to describe the sights. In the following case, students looked at pictures of autumn leaves. Then they were asked to generate action words that described the movements of the leaves.

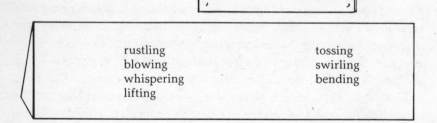

rustling	tossing
blowing	swirling
whispering	bending
lifting	

Finally, the students created descriptive passages by using the action words in phrases, thus translating their visual experiences into literature. (This exercise works both orally and in writing.)

golden leaves rustling in the wind

blowing, swirling leaves lifting upward

painted leaves whispering in the forest

An alternative would be to create a chart of leaf characteristics that would show students the different elements of what they see. This exercise could easily be incorporated into a science lesson about different leaves and tree species.

	COLOR	TEXTURE	SIZE	SHAPE	CONDITION
LEAVES	golden	shiny	large	elongated	brittle
	fiery	worn	tiny	oval	aged
	red	scratchy		pointed	crumpled
	radiant	wrinkled			

Picture Summaries

In this activity, students find a picture or photograph from a magazine that best expresses the theme of a story or book they are reading. This helps readers to process text and search for deeper interpretations as they respond to a literary selection. Sharing in a small group, each student can discuss the links between the meaning of the picture he or she has chosen and a theme from the story. As they share aesthetically, students respond emotionally by identifying with the story characters and reacting personally to the literary selection. If you keep a supply of old magazines in the classroom and replenish it regularly, students will have a rich source of pictures to choose from. The activity works best with older students, who are more adept at generalizing and linking themes.

For Developing Learners: The universal theme of friendship and loyalty in E. B. White's *Charlotte's Web* may be apparent to most young readers but students need to relate this theme to themselves by making connections to their own life experiences.

A grade four student selected a magazine picture to discuss the concept of teamwork, a subtheme of the story. Justin, age ten, explained how Wilbur, Templeton, and Charlotte each had very special abilities and each in their own way was a team member, able to loyally support one another whenever in need. The picture he chose had nothing to do with pigs or spiders: it showed four crew members working together to moor their boat.

This picture makes me think of how Charlotte, Wilbur, and Templeton all worked together as a team to help one another. Both Charlotte and Templeton were Wilbur's friends. Charlotte was the unselfish one and Templeton was the greedy friend. Some people don't like Templeton but he was loyal. He helped when he was asked to. He got scraps of paper so that Charlotte could write words and he rescued Charlotte's sac of eggs.

Viewing the World

Having brainstormed descriptive and action words to interpret images, students can expand their ideas independently in personal writing while viewing anything from puddles or streams to busy city streets. If you are out on a field trip, why not give students a little time to record their reactions to what they see? The following poems were written by students in a grade three class while viewing a waterfall in a mountain canyon.

The Waterfall

Waterfalls crashing
Thundering noise
Water flowing rapidly
Carving rock
Kids looking from a cave
Watching closely
A bride's veil.

   Lora

Memories of the Canyon

Roaring waterfalls,
Churning plunge pools,
Looking from the cave with
 wet mist,
Hiking through the forest,
Lots of green,
Giant trees,
The deep blue "Ink Pots",
Rushing water,
The faces of the mountains,
Looking down upon the
 valley.

   Alison

Such writing is the epitome of whole language learning: language itself becomes part of an experience that is both sensory and emotional. This integration of language and life experience lies at the core of making meaning, and as we will see in the next chapter, the same integration should be part of reading.

CHAPTER THREE

Reading

Making meaning lies at the heart of all language, and that includes language. But before we examine the substance of reading, it is important to look at its forms. Students' early experiences with reading will radically affect their level of comfort and ability. For that reason, the way in which you as a teacher introduce them to reading is vital. Shared reading — sharing a book with a group — allows everyone to become involved in a story without feeling pressured to "perform" alone. It is a wonderful way to begin. Silent, individual reading has its own power, but it comes later.

Shared Reading

Reading aloud is an important way of sharing books with children. It develops and enriches their language while at the same time building concepts about reading and writing. You can read and reread books, inviting students to participate in the reading in a number of ways. One popular method today is the use of "Big Books" with reading groups. These Big Books — with large type and illustrations — allow groups of students to actively participate in viewing and talking about illustrations and text. Whether you use them or not, when sharing reading with your class, you should try to replicate the intimate adult-child interactions that are part of bedtime story-reading at home. Shared reading can accomplish this through a variety of group activities.

Choral Reading

Choral reading allows students to read aloud within the safety of a group. Long before fluent reading ability is developed, students can experiment with the sounds and rhythms of language. Many students who cannot read independently can join in by participating in repeating lines or taking part in reciting verses they know from memory. The sound of the text is as important as the visual text in learning to read. Students need the security of hearing the text to become accustomed to book language.

You can organize choral reading in several ways: the whole class can read in unison, or different groups or individuals can read particular lines from the text. Older readers can experiment with the tempo or rhythm in a variety of oral arrangements.

- **Antiphonal:** Students are divided into two or more alternate speaking groups and each group reads a part of the text.
- **Refrain:** One reader reads the main part of the text and the group reads the refrain or repeating lines in unison.
- **Cumulative:** Students are divided into several groups. One group begins reading and is joined by each group one by one until everyone is participating.

Echo Reading

Echo reading is a form of assisted reading in which students repeat phrases or sentences after the person who is doing the reading aloud. While reading, students follow the print from a Big Book, chart, overhead projector, or chalkboard. This encourages them to memorize any rhythmic language in the text while at the same time working out the connection between print and speech. Echo reading works well with beginning, ESL, or linguistically different readers who should memorize and rehearse the text before tackling it independently.

Readers' Theatre

Readers' theatre is a dramatic interpretation of a script or a literary selection through a group reading. Students use voice and gesture to convey the ideas and moods of a particular story. Stories that have generous dialogue are the best choice for readers' theatre.

Simultaneous Listening and Reading

Students read along with a story on a tape or record. (Give them many opportunities to read and listen repeatedly to the same story until they can read it fluently on their own.) Many publishers produce tapes and records with their books. If a favorite book is not available on tape, you can make your own.

For Beginning Readers: For all kinds of shared reading, choose books that have rhythmic and playful language, such as Ellen Bryan Obed's poems in *Wind in My Pocket:*

> Witchgrass, stitchgrass, in-the-roadside-ditch-grass;
> Junegrass, strewngrass, waving-on-the-dune grass. . .

Other good choices include: Joanne Oppenheim's *You Can't Catch Me!*, Elizabeth Winthrop's *Sledding*, Ann Rockwell's *Thump, Thump, Thump!*, Janet Stevens's edition of Edward Lear's *The Owl and the Pussycat*, or her own story, *The House That Jack Built*, Robert Wyndham's *Chinese Mother Goose Rhymes*, Jill Bennett's *Noisy Poems*, Bill Martin Jr. and John Archambault's *Listen to the Rain* and *Barn Dance*, Peter Eyvindson's *Circus Berserkus*, and Arnold Lobel's *The Rose in My Garden* or *The Book of Pigerick: Pig Limericks.*

For Developing Readers: Older students can interpret the sounds or moods of language by experimenting with antiphonal or rhythmic arrangements of poetry as in Paul Fleischmann's *Joyful Noises: Poems for Two Voices*, Susan Jeffers's illustrated version of Longfellow's *Hiawatha* or Robert Frost's *Stopping by Woods on a Snowy Evening*, Byrd Baylor's *The Other Way to Listen*, or Diane Stanley's edition of James Whitcomb Riley's *Little Orphant Annie*. Other possibilities include chanting the onomatopoeic Japanese words in Momoko Ishii's *The Tongue-tied Sparrow*, interpreting the Appalachian dialect in Lois Lowry's *Rabble Starkey*, or trying Charles Keller's *Tongue Twisters*, a challenge for mature readers.

Silent Reading

A very important part of reading in whole language classrooms lies in selecting something to read and sustaining silent reading long enough to make meaning and derive pleasure from the reading material. Some students may not have "quiet times" at home to enjoy literary selections, so they never read entire books or respond to literature in a personal way. During silent reading in school, they can choose their own books rather than just being assigned readings. No matter how good or poor their skills are, encourage them to "read" as best they can and try to figure out words independently.

In a good silent reading program:

- Readers seek out books by favorite authors and illustrators.
- Readers read for their own pleasure.
- Readers reread favorite books.
- Readers discuss books with their friends and exchange opinions on good books to read.
- Readers share their books in a number of informal ways.

Here are two ways to encourage students to share their own reading with each other.

Book Talks

As important as a time for reading is a time for talking about books. Book talks put reading in a social context, allowing students to share their reading with classmates either in pairs or in a group. Their primary purpose is to interest other classmates in reading the book themselves, but they also help students to exchange reactions and feelings towards a literary selection rather than generate a "right answer". Emphasis should be on the reader's interpretation of the literary selection rather than on comprehension. Variation in individual responses to books should

29

be expected and encouraged. Students can make pop-ups or dioramas to advertize their favorite books.

Word Collector's Chair

Some students like to highlight a book talk by sharing the special language that an author uses — catchy words or phrases, story beginnings, refrains, rhymes, etc. They may note the way an author vividly describes a character, the setting, or an action in a story. You may want to set up a special place or chair for sharing such discoveries.

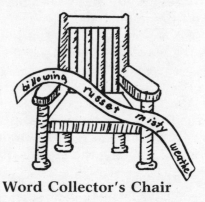

Word Collector's Chair

Wordless Picture Books

Wordless picture books can be "read", even though they tell stories purely through pictures, and they deserve special mention here. Each story unfolds as the reader views the gestures, facial expressions, and the action of the characters and the story setting. These books can be used for encouraging reading readiness, developing oral language, and motivating creative writing. They are also valuable for group activities as they permit students of different language abilities to enjoy the same book. Students can expand their oral vocabularies by narrating such a story.

Wordless books invite individual interpretations. Some wordless books contain easily identifiable plots that students can narrate individually or collaboratively. Others lend themselves to numerous story interpretations.

For Beginning Readers: A good beginning story would be Brinton Turkel's *Deep in the Forest*, which reverses the plot of Grimm's *Goldilocks and the Three Bears*. If you read *Goldilocks* to your students first, they will have prior knowledge of both the story plot and language, and so will usually be able to narrate the story quite fluently.

Caution: Since most wordless picture books contain contemporary story plots that may be unknown to your students, you may want to construct wordless Big Books to use for additional practice with stories that are familiar. A simple solution would be to have older students illustrate some traditional tales such as *The Three Little Pigs, Little Red Riding Hood,* or *The Gingerbread Boy* as Big Books. These "homemade" books can be used in shared reading if you ask students to narrate the stories. Tomie de Paola's *Pancakes for Breakfast* is excellent for helping beginners develop a story sequence, as the plot is simple. Wordless books such as Mercer Mayer's *Frog on His Own*, Peter Spier's *Rain*, or Raymond Briggs's *The Snowman* are intermediate books. They can be used after students have had some experience viewing the pictures and building the story sequence.

For Developing Readers: With their colorful illustrations wordless books can motivate older students to write individual stories or group stories. Chris Van Allsburg's almost wordless *The Mysteries of Harris Burdick* or Remy Charlip and Jerry Joyner's *Thirteen* can invite a multitude of interpretations.

Now that your students are reading — together or alone — it is vital that you begin to monitor what they are making of it, what they are getting out of it.

Evaluating Reading Comprehension

Reading comprehension is an active process that involves making meaning. Every text provides cues that help the reader to construct a personal meaning, and the reader builds that meaning by connecting *new* knowledge to *prior* knowledge, not only of the world but also of the structure of texts. Narrative and expository texts are organized in different ways, and as your students develop as readers, they will gain insights about texts that will make their learning easier.

But how do you know what meaning your students are making of their reading? As is the case with so much teaching, the simplest way to find out is to ask them questions.

Asking Questions

Good questioning will not only help you in evaluating comprehension, but also lead to more effective comprehension. And, of course, there are many different kinds of questions varying widely in degrees of abstraction and conceptual difficulty.

The use of questioning can be applied to Byrd Baylor's *Hawk, I'm Your Brother*, a realistic story about Rudy Soto, a young Native boy, and his dream of flying like a hawk.

- **Literal comprehension** questions require readers to relate what the author said, and usually the number of possible answers is limited (e.g., "Where does the story take place?").
- **Inferential comprehension** questions require readers to infer an answer from the facts in the text (e.g., "What message do you think the author, Byrd Baylor, was trying to communicate?"). The readers must "read between the lines", but should be able to justify their answers. Response justifications give teachers insight into their students' thinking.
- **Experientially based comprehension** questions require readers to use the facts in a text in conjunction with prior knowledge and experiences to derive logical inferences from the text (e.g., "Can you tell why you would like to have Rudy Soto as a good friend?"). Experiential questions help students to accommodate new information and extend their knowledge by relating the content of the text to personal experiences.

Questioning follows naturally after students have read a story. Encourage students to respond to it but refrain from "testing" them. What matters is that you guide students to make personal responses and to use specific parts of the text to support their reactions.

For Beginning Readers: Ask younger students, "Did anything in the story especially interest you? Surprise you? Frighten you?"

Have students compare their experiences of the text with their real-life experiences.

For Developing Readers: Ask older students, "What pictures do you get in your mind of this character, setting, or event? If you went to the place where your story took place, what would you see?"

When to Question

You may have to ask questions at all stages of any reading. If you plan your questions, you can effectively guide the interactions between reader and text.

Before Reading: Set students' thinking in motion by activating their prior knowledge about a topic covered in the text. Guide them to look at the book's cover, title, and illustrations. Then activate their thinking about the story's meaning by asking, "What do you think this story is about?"

During Reading: Focus students' attention by directing their thoughts to selected aspects of a text. Help them to integrate the meaning while reading by stopping at several intervals in the text and asking them to predict the plot: "What do you think will happen next?"

After Reading: Monitor students' comprehension by checking their understanding of certain aspects of the text. The emphasis of post-reading comprehension questions should be on connecting ideas rather than on simply rehashing the text. Give students an opportunity to check out their predictions by asking, "Did the story turn out the way you expected it would?" or, "Would you like to change it in any way?"

Whole language teachers guide reflective discussions of literary selections after students have read a story. As with listening, the best questions are those that help students to think about what the story has meant to them.

Some Considerations about Questions

- Good questioning abilities develop over time. Make sure you don't ask too many literal questions, as students need to process text information beyond just what the author says if they are to understand it in any meaningful way. Questions need to be asked at all levels of comprehension, so that students have an opportunity to think about the text in terms they might not imagine on their own.

Questions such as, "What is the main idea?" or, "What kind of person is the main character in the story?" will probably require readers to synthesize the facts in a story in order to arrive at an answer. Questions beginning with the phrase "Do you think. . ." will likely elicit more personal, experientially based responses. The latter kind of question will lead to deeper understanding.

- Give students the freedom to make divergent responses. They may give plausible responses that are different from those you might have considered. Encourage and nurture personal interpretations of literature.

- Students need time to think about their responses. Giving them more time to respond to questions promotes longer, more accurate, and more speculative responses.

Caution: Questioning is not the only way to assess reading comprehension. If a student can restate the main idea from a literary text in another form such as art, music, writing, storytelling, or drama, then you know that the student has understood it.

Predicting Plots

Like good listeners, good readers use context clues and their own prior knowledge to make predictions while they are reading. Using what is called a reading-thinking strategy, ask readers to predict what will come next in a story, using clues to justify those predictions; reading to confirm, reject, or modify predictions; and making or adjusting new predictions. Books that have predictable plots can be used to encourage students to actively think about and make inferences about plot development.

For Beginning Readers: The repetitive patterns of Audrey Wood's *King Bidgood's in the Bathtub*, Nonny Hogrogian's *The Cat Who Loved to Sing*, Sarah Barchas's *I Was Walking down the Road*, or Merle Peek's *Mary Wore Her Red Dress and Harold Wore His*

Green Sneakers invite beginning readers to predict what will happen next.

With books that may not have a repetitive pattern, prediction can be modeled by stopping at interesting parts of the story and asking students, "What do you think will happen next?" Mildred Pitts Walter's *Brother to the Wind* and Arthur Yorinks's *Hey Al* are exciting and suspenseful stories that will help encourage readers to predict the plots.

For Developing Readers: Older students can identify foreshadowing, a literary device that suggests or predicts plot development through illustrations, mood, choice of words, or changing events. As students read, they search for clues that foreshadow what may happen next.

Students can use the author's clues to predict Sam's mishaps in Lois Lowry's *All about Sam*, how changes in attitudes may affect Jeff in Cynthia Voigt's *A Solitary Blue*, or the adventures and misadventures of the two runaways, Prince Brat and Jemmy, who exchange identities in Sid Fleischman's *The Whipping Boy*.

What Are the Purposes of Reading?

Reading has two main purposes: *enjoyment* and *gaining information*. And it is important to remember that non-fiction can be read for enjoyment, fiction for information. Both literary forms should be part of your reading programs. And although the activities outlined in the rest of this chapter appear under "Reading for Enjoyment" or "Reading for Information", they can all be applied to both.

Reading for Enjoyment

As students read stories, they develop an understanding of themselves and others as they relate to story characters or happenings. They also develop an awareness of the organizational patterns of story. This awareness is called a "concept of story", and it includes information about the structural elements of stories: plot, setting, character, theme, and point of view. A concept of story is essential if students are to be successful as both readers and writers.

One way to develop an understanding of story structure is by reading and comparing different stories. Critical reading skills develop when students make literary connections between stories they have read and enjoyed.

Story Variation

Many stories are "intertextually linked", having similar patterns that can be compared. After listening to a number of literary selections, students can visualize and relate story connections by examining plots, settings, characters, or themes. Teachers can assist in making story connections by posing interpretative questions:

- Does this story remind you of any other story?
- Is this story character like any other character you have read about?

Observing the many possible variations of a theme, for instance, can help students see the ways different writers "weave" similar ideas.

For Beginning Readers: Younger students can compare stories such as the following:

"AFRAID OF THE DARK" STORIES:
Paulette Bourgeois's *Franklin in the Dark*
Robert Crowe's *Clyde Monster*
Mercer Mayer's *There's a Nightmare in My Closet* and
   There's an Alligator under My Bed

"ALWAYS ROOM FOR ONE MORE" STORIES:
Audrey Wood's *The Napping House*
Jan Brett's *The Mitten*
Margot Zemach's *It Could Always Be Worse*
Joanna Cole's *It's Too Noisy*
Ann McGovern's *Too Much Noise*
Ruth Brown's *The Big Sneeze*

IMAGINARY JOURNEYS:
Hiawayan Orm's *In the Attic* and
                    Ned and the Jaybaloo.
Joan Blos's *Lottie's Circus*
Rafe Martin's *Will's Mammoth*
Eugenie Fernandez's *A Difficult Day*
Maurice Sendak's *Where the Wild Things Are*
Chris Van Allsburg's *The Polar Express*
Jan Wahl's *Humphrey's Bear*
Allan Morgan's *Nicole's Boat*

"CINDERELLA" STORIES:
Shirley Climo's *The Egyptian Cinderella* (Egyptian)
Joseph Jacob's *Tattercoats* (English)
Charlotte Huck's *Princess Furball* (North American)
William Hooks's *Moss Gown* (North American)
Virginia Haviland's *The Indian Cinderella* (Native American)
Robert San Souci's *The Talking Eggs* (Creole)
John Steptoe's *Mufaro's Beautiful Daughters: An African Tale*
    (Zimbabwean)
Ann Nolan Clark's *In the Land of Small Dragon* (Vietnamese)
Lynette Dyer Vuong's *The Brocaded Slipper and Other Viet-
    namese Tales* (Vietnamese)
Ai-Ling Louie's *Yeh-Shen: A Cinderella Story from China*
    (Chinese)

For Developing Readers: Older students can compare the
theme of cooperation as it is developed in Jean Craighead
George's *Julie of the Wolves* with Laura Ingalls Wilder's *Little
House in the Big Woods*, or shyness as portrayed in Maria Gripe's
Elvis and His Secret and Mary Calhoun's *Julie Tree.*

They can also link story characters, comparing their similari-
ties and their differences. Ask them to use a Venn diagram to
compare how dreams changed for Aremis Slake in Felice Holman's *Slake's Limbo* and for Milo Critchley in Stephen Manes's
Be a Perfect Person in Just Three Days.

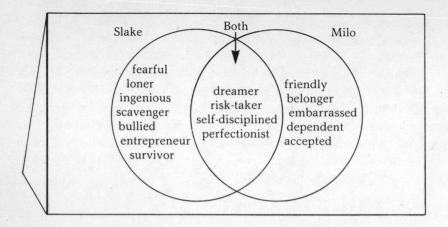

The potential list of comparisons is endless. You can compare Emma's struggles for independence in Louise Fitzhugh's *Nobody's Family Is Going to Change* with Jasmin's in Jan Truss's *Jasmin*. Or compare Willy, who accepts the responsibility of saving his grandfather's farm in John Gardiner's *Stone Fox*, with Dewey, who saves his grandmother in Betsy Byars's *Trouble River*.

Finally, older readers might discuss how animals help story characters discover something about themselves by comparing Willie in Betsy Byars's *Midnight Fox* with Link in Keith Robertson's *In Search of a Sandhill Crane* or Gaspard in Donn Kushner's *The Violin Maker's Gift*.

Reading for Information

One of the most important aspects of any whole language program should be the use of literature across the curriculum. Nonfiction books that relate to science, social studies, or the arts provide students with information and answers to their questions about their world. They encourage students to seek answers as they investigate phenomena, whether deserts, storms, animals, weather, or ballet.

Luckily, there is a trend towards non-fiction texts covering a wider variety of topics and formats, often with detailed drawings, photographs, or three-dimensional aids such as wheels, foldouts, or pop-ups. For teachers who want to be aware of recent publications there are two annual reviews of new books in science and social studies. *Outstanding Science Trade Books for Children* is published in *Science and Children*, and *Notable Children's Trade Books in the Field of Social Studies* appears in *Social Education*.

Non-fiction does present readers with some special challenges. It often includes unfamiliar vocabulary or new concepts. Strategies that can help facilitate reading comprehension of non-fiction need to be modeled and practised. Like the directed reading thinking activity in fiction, these strategies will help students improve their understanding and retention of the information.

Strategies for Reading Non-fiction

Students may be less intimidated by non-fiction if you suggest they do some of the following:

- Develop a purpose for reading.
- Scan the book to see if it contains the sort of information you want or need.
- Skim it to get an overview of the content: introduction, headings, graphics, summary.
- Make predictions about what the author will say.
- Use pictures, other graphics, and cloze reading to confirm predictions.
- Stop reading when you lose track of the meaning.
- Apply "think-alouds" (see below) to gain understanding.
- Tie the ideas in the text to existing knowledge while you read.
- Reflect on what you have learned from the text.

Think-alouds

These are a kind of comprehension monitoring strategy in which readers consciously question their own understanding by asking themselves, "Am I making sense?" Students learn to verbalize their ongoing mental processes and reasoning behavior to gain understanding. Teachers can model this think-aloud strategy through explicit instruction by showing how syntactic and semantic clues help readers make educated guesses about the meanings of unknown words. In short, readers learn to be problem-solvers.

The following suggestions should help students who are having trouble understanding.

When in difficulty:
- Skip unknown word and read ahead to get more information.
  "I'll read ahead to get more information."
- Make a guess based on prior knowledge and content.
  "The rest of the sentence makes me think it means _____."
- Reread to clarify ideas.
  "I'll reread and try again."
- Reread and question the text.
  "I'll reread and ask myself what is happening here."
- Replace the unknown word with a synonym.
  "I'll replace the word with one that I think will fit."
- Make an analogy by linking prior knowledge with new information.
  "This is like a _____, which is something I already know."
- Organize images by making a mental picture.
  "As I read I'll paint a picture and guess what's missing. . ."

Semantic Webs

If a reader is to understand a non-fiction text — or, indeed, *any* text — there must be a bridge between the reader's prior knowledge and the ideas communicated in the text. Helping readers organize what they know and showing them where and how ideas are related are essential for meaningful learning. Key concepts or main ideas can be displayed on a chart in a diagram or semantic web as readers clarify their thinking before reading a book. Semantic webs can be drawn to illustrate any concept. Instruction begins with the teacher asking questions, but after a while, students will be able to initiate their own productions.

For instance, before reading Dorothy Paten's *Spider Magic*, ask students to discuss what they already know about the topic and predict what they want to learn. The results might look like this:

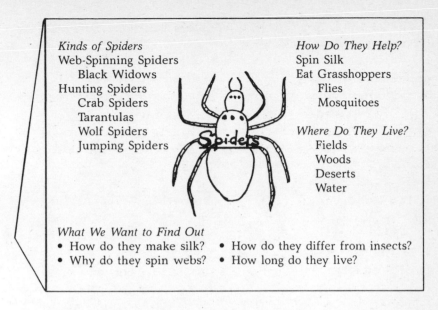

Kinds of Spiders	How Do They Help?
Web-Spinning Spiders	Spin Silk
Black Widows	Eat Grasshoppers
Hunting Spiders	Flies
Crab Spiders	Mosquitoes
Tarantulas	
Wolf Spiders	Where Do They Live?
Jumping Spiders	Fields
	Woods
	Deserts
	Water

What We Want to Find Out
- How do they make silk?
- Why do they spin webs?
- How do they differ from insects?
- How long do they live?

After reading, students should discuss what they have read and relate or add new information to the semantic web.

Across-the-Curriculum Reading

Across-the-curriculum reading is just that. You choose themes, and within these themes students read literature for research, for relating it to other subjects, and for recreation. In choosing a theme there should be a balance between non-fiction that will build background and fiction that might include poetry and songs.

For Beginning Readers: Using spiders as a theme, a good beginning selection would be Eric Carle's fictional *The Very Busy Spider*, which is an introduction to how a spider builds and uses a web. A complementary text about a spider who takes spinning seriously, is Jenny Wagner's *Aranea: A Story about a Spider*, or Shirley Climo's spider who spins a Christmas surprise in *The Cobweb Christmas*.

For Developing Readers: Informational texts are a major resource for the science and social studies curriculum. Claudia Schnieper's *Amazing Spiders*, Margaret Lane's *The Spider*, Tom Walther's *A Spider Might*, and Alex Crosby's *Tarantulas: The Biggest Spiders* allow students to expand their knowledge about

FICTION
Picture Storybooks
   Cobweb Christmas
   Spiders in the Fruit Cellar
   Tales of an Ashanti Father
   The Adventures of Spider
   The Web in the Grass
   Aranea: A Story about a Spider
   The Very Busy Spider

Junior Novels
   Charlotte's Web
   Like Jake and Me

NON-FICTION
   Amazing Spiders
   A First Look at Spiders
   Someone Saw a Spider
   Tarantulas: The Biggest Spider
   The Spider
   A Spider Might
   Spider Magic

ART
Bookmaking
   Borders
   Endpapers
   Collage
   Cut Paper
   Paper Engineering
   Painting
   Printmaking
   Scratchboard
   Stitchery

VIEWING
Sensory Viewing
   Picture Books
   Slides
   Nature
Brainstorming
   Sensory Language
Picture Summaries

MUSIC
   Ballads
   Musical Dramatizations
   Singing

DRAMA
   Dramatizing Stories
   Improvisation
   Mime
   Role-playing
   Storytelling

POETRY
The Spider's Dance
Don't Eat Spiders

READING
Choral Reading
Readers' Theatre
Book Talks
Word Collector's Chair
Reading Strategies for Non-
   Fiction
Think-alouds
Semantic Webs
Predicting Plots

WRITING
DESCRIPTION
Story Beginnings
Word Pictures
   Character Sketches
   Setting Sketches
EXPOSITION
Eye Witness News Reports
Research Reports
EXPRESSION
Advice Column
Autobiography
Learning Log
Letters to the Editor
Letters to Story Characters
NARRATION
Legend
Mystery
Myth
Tall Tale
Trickster Tale
PERSUASION
Advertisement
Editorial
POETRY
Cinquain
Free Verse
Shape

LISTENING/TALKING
Personal Sharing/Responding
Group Sharing
Oral Cloze
Anticipating Future Actions/Events
Title/Headline Summary

spiders while at the same time practising non-fiction reading strategies. Extending the range of student interest could include E.B. White's novel *Charlotte's Web*; Joanne Ryder's poetic text, *The Spider's Dance*; Joyce Cooper Arhurst's West African tales, *The Adventures of Spider*; Barbara Joosse's realistic fiction of over-coming fears of spiders in *Spiders in the Fruit Cellar*; or a family story about an incident with a wolf spider which bonds a young boy with his stepfather in Mavis Jukes's *Like Jake and Me*.

A spider theme could include a range of possible integrated activities, as illustrated on pages 42-43 (a full list of spider books appears in the bibliography at the end of this book). Of course, you will want to tailor your choice of theme to the interests and needs of your students. And whatever your theme, you may choose a particular "language focus": reading, writing, speaking, etc.

Note that the web diagram includes not only activities we have already examined — listening, talking, viewing, and reading — but also writing, art, music, and drama. We turn now to all of the latter.

CHAPTER FOUR

Writing

As with reading, the ultimate goal of writing is to make meaning, and the development of any writing program should depend upon the needs of the students as they try to effectively communicate their ideas in a variety of contexts. There should be a balance between writing in both assigned and unassigned tasks, each with its own merits. In assigned writing tasks, teachers can specify the writing form, but students should choose their own topics within that form. In unassigned tasks, students choose their own writing forms and topics, learning to express ideas creatively without anxiety over adhering to a "correct" writing form.

Through concrete experiences, reading and listening to literature, and learning about the structures of different writing forms, students develop ways to communicate for a variety of purposes and audiences. It is essential that *many* literary forms be shared and discussed with students before they write. As they become familiar with and internalize many types of literature, they will experiment with these forms in their own writing. Students should use writing to describe, to narrate, to explain, to persuade, to inquire, to inform, and to express feelings. There are many ways to categorize the writing forms that suit these purposes, and it is possible to do so too rigidly: sometimes students may combine more than one form in a single piece of writing. Generally, however, the form a text should take is determined by the purpose of the text and its intended audience. In other words, what does the writer want to say, and to whom? is it, for instance, a letter to a friend, or a research report for a teacher? The diagram below indicates the broad variety of forms writers can use. All will be dealt with in this chapter, ranging from the simplest to the most difficult. If you want any of these activities to lead to making actual books, information about putting them together is included in the chapter on art.

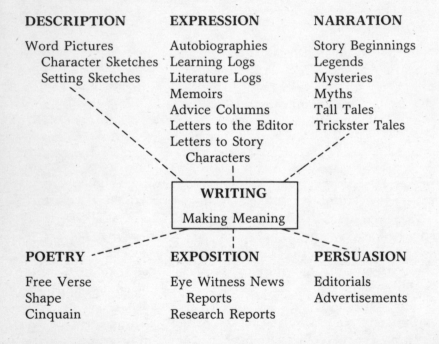

DESCRIPTION

Word Pictures
   Character Sketches
   Setting Sketches

EXPRESSION

Autobiographies
Learning Logs
Literature Logs
Memoirs
Advice Columns
Letters to the Editor
Letters to Story
   Characters

NARRATION

Story Beginnings
Legends
Mysteries
Myths
Tall Tales
Trickster Tales

WRITING

Making Meaning

POETRY

Free Verse
Shape
Cinquain

EXPOSITION

Eye Witness News
   Reports
Research Reports

PERSUASION

Editorials
Advertisements

Description

Good descriptive writing creates a picture for the reader. It can describe anything from a setting to characters to feelings, and it is part of virtually every form of writing, from fiction to nonfiction, prose to poetry, drama, some lyrics, and more. For that reason, I begin with activities designed to enhance students' skills in description: these skills will stand them in good stead no matter what writing form they choose to work in.

Word Pictures

Word pictures create an interest in language without putting the demands on students that story writing involves. Show students a slide or picture from a literary selection and then ask what words they can suggest to "paint a picture in your head". Students then write a word picture. The visual stimuli are the primary source of the word pictures. Words are secondary and refer to what has been perceived through the senses. These word pictures can be sketches that describe either a setting or a character, and they can evolve into texts that become stories.

Setting Sketches

A story's setting in time and space helps readers share the story's characters' experiences. Authors use settings to create places or moods which add credibility to a story's plot and characters.

There are two main types of settings in literature. The first is the "backdrop setting", which is barely sketched. Many folktales use "Once upon a time. . ." or "Long ago and far away. . ." as the only clue to their setting. More contemporary authors such as Jane Yolen lightly sketch the setting using a few more details, as in *Silent Bianca*: "Once far to the North, where the world is lighted only by the softly flickering snow. . ."

The second type is the "integral setting", which is more vivid in its elaboration. Physical details are clear so that readers understand how the story is related to a time and place. The forest setting in Margery Williams's *The Velveteen Rabbit* illustrates how images can be painted with words for younger readers.

> It was light now, for the moon had risen.
> All the forest was beautiful and the fronds of the
> bracken shone like frosted silver.

Lively descriptions of the Canadian North are also detailed for older readers in Farley Mowat's *Lost in the Barrens*, or the Nova Scotia landscape in Paula Fox's *The Moonlight Man*. After reading a number of such vivid descriptions, students can then write word pictures from a text of their choice.

For Beginning Writers: Younger students can use the detailed illustrations in picture books as a writing stimulus. After reading Tomie dePaola's *The Legend of the Bluebonnet*, a grade three student writes about the sight of bluebonnets in this way:

> A field of bluebonnets. Blue and fragrant petals, lazily blowing in the breeze, sprouting endlessly across the fields, and in time covering the earth with a delicate beauty.

For Developing Writers: Older students can describe the locked garden in Frances Hodgson Burnett's *The Secret Garden*, the magical forest setting in Dennis Haseley's *My Father Doesn't Know about the Woods and Me*, the Catskill wilderness in Jean Craighead George's *My Side of the Mountain*, or the surrealistic garden of Chris Van Allsburg's *The Garden of Abdul Gasazi.*

Character Sketches

Authors develop story characters through physical description, dialogue, action, inner thoughts, and/or simile and metaphor. All are worth exploring with your students.

PHYSICAL DESCRIPTION

Characters can be described using descriptions of the way they appear. The details and vocabulary need not be dry: not all children's literature is characterized by concise or repetitive language; some writers use more interesting and colorful language to express their ideas. Patricia Pendergraf crafts vivid character descriptions in *Hear the Wind Blow* and Leslie Kimmelman's Frannie verbally sketches family and customers who visit her family's produce stand in *Frannie's Fruits.*

Using literary examples, students can, for instance, be shown how several authors describe similar characters, each in a different way. The following passages all describe characters who are old.

Miska Miles describes the grandmother in *Annie and the Old One:*

> A web of wrinkles criss-crossed her face.

Margery Williams selects certain details to describe the Skin Horse in *The Velveteen Rabbit:*

He was so old his fur was bald in patches and he was coming apart at the seams.

Shirley Climo's Tante from *The Cobweb Christmas* is described in such a way that readers must form their own images:

She was so old she couldn't count all the Christmases she had seen.

Try asking your students to select a favorite story character that is lightly sketched by the author and add more physical details to describe that character.

For Beginning Writers: Younger writers can use existing details along with their own additions to create a fuller description of Rosa from Vera Williams's *Something Special for Me*; Willaby, the sensitive first grader in Rachel Isadora's *Willaby*; Alistair Grittle from Marilyn Sadler's *Alistair's Elephant*; or Samantha, the imaginative heroine of Evaline Ness's *Sam, Bangs and Moonshine.*

For Developing Writers: Older students can describe Chibi from Taro Yashima's *Crow Boy*, shy Julie from May Calhoun's *Julie's Tree*, Anna from Jean Little's *From Anna* or Ben in Little's *Different Dragons*, Pete from Cynthia Rylant's *A Fine White Dust*, or the courageous Billie Wind from Jean George's *The Talking Earth.*

DIALOGUE

Readers also learn about characters by reading what they say and how they say it. Dialogue helps to develop characters and to move the plot forward. Sharon Bell Mathis, for instance, reveals Great-aunt Dew's character in *The Hundred Penny Box* in an episode when she talks about the old box in which she keeps a penny for every year of her life: "When I lose my hundred penny box, I lose me."

To help students respond to the feelings, beliefs, and motives of a story character — their own or someone else's — you may want them to create an imaginary conversation that the character might have. This could take the form of a cartoon strip, a soliloquy, a letter to another story character, or a diary entry.

For Beginning Writers: Younger writers could write a conversation that Emery Raccoon from Marjorie Weinman Sharmat's *The 329th Friend* could have explaining his plans for a very nice day; or Franklin, the turtle, from Paulette Bourgeois's *Franklin in the Dark*, explaining how comfortable he feels in his shell at night.

For Developing Writers: A suggestion for older students would be to have Alex Frankovitch talk about his life as a star doing cat food commercials in Barbara Park's *Skinnybones* and *Almost Starring Skinnybones*; or Aremis Slake discuss a frightening experience while living in the tunnel on his own in Felice Holman's *Slake's Limbo*.

ACTIONS

What a story character does and the way he or she does it gives readers insights into that character. In Betsy Byars's *Trouble River*, readers can infer Dewey's character as he is described in the escape episode in which he, his grandmother, and Charlie, the dog, float down the river on a handmade raft:

> He hugged the dog to him. He had the lonely feeling that he and Grandma and Charlie were the only living creatures left in the world, and he buried his face in the dog's fur and waited until the tears in his eyes had dried.

Ask your students to think of words that describe a character's actions and record them in a list of character traits. In the process, they will come to understand how characters' actions reveal personality traits.

Opposite is a student example of a list of character traits about Sarah from Patricia MacLachlan's *Sarah Plain and Tall*. Some of the adjectives may not seem to follow from the actions; if not, you have a good opportunity to ask questions that lead to discussion and clarification of the student's reasoning.

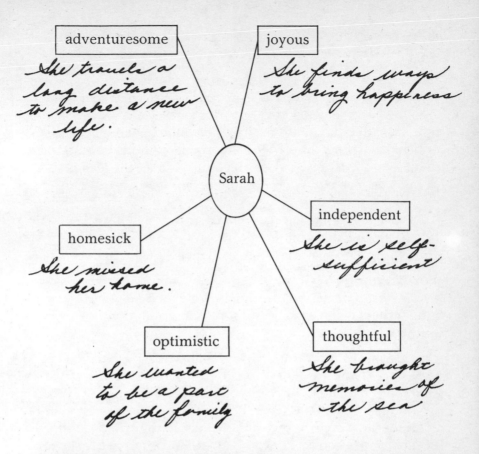

adventuresome — *She travels a long distance to make a new life.*

joyous — *She finds ways to bring happiness*

Sarah

independent — *She is self-sufficient*

homesick — *She missed her home.*

optimistic — *She wanted to be a part of the family*

thoughtful — *She brought memories of the sea*

For Beginning Writers: Younger students can generate words to describe the actions of Jan Andrews's Eva from *Very Last First Time*, Su Ann and Kevin Kiser's Timothy in *The Birthday Thing*, or Katie from Ian Wallace's *The Sparrow's Song*, and contribute their ideas to a group chart.

For Developing Writers: Some suggestions for older writers could include thinking of adjectives or phrases that describe the actions of Benjy in Betsy Byars's *The Eighteenth Emergency*, Rachel from Norma Fox Mazer's *After the Rain*, Leona in Juanita Havill's *It Always Happens to Leona*, Kit Fox from Jan Hudson's *Dawn Rider*, Wanda from Eleanor Estes's *The Hundred Dresses*, Michael from Kevin Major's *Hold Fast*, Jeremy from Jean Little's *Mama's Going to Buy You a Mockingbird*, or Ned in Paula Fox's *One-Eyed Cat*.

These, of course, reveal much about characters' motives, feelings, and ideas. Cora Taylor describes Julie Morgan's inner feelings when she talks to a tree about her first day of school.

> It's the first day that I'm scared of, Julie explained. . . saying the wrong things. . . knowing something I shouldn't know. . . There was a deep sigh through all the leaves and the tree was still again. Julie felt sadder than tears.

As writers begin to develop characters through physical description, dialogue, and action, encourage them to explore alternate ways to develop characters through inner thoughts and responses.

For Beginning Writers: After reading about Frankie Valdez's perception of his birthday in Tricia Brown's *Hello Amigos!*, beginning writers can try using a first-person point of view in stories of their own.

For Developing Writers: More skilled writers may want to explore a "you are there" feeling by having their own story characters explain their points of view with a variety of literary techniques. Lucille Clifton, for instance, uses a stream-of-consciousness style to reveal the young heroine in *Sonora Beautiful*; readers watch Kit grow as Barbara Corcoran uses first-person narration in *I Am the Universe*; Blue, the fisherman's dog, tells the story in Patricia Wrightson's *Moon Dark*; Louise is the storyteller in Katherine Paterson's *Jacob Have I Loved*; a simulated journal chronicles Catherine's story in Joan Blos's *A Gathering of Days: A New England Girl's Journal 1830-1832*; while the ten Rosso children tell their story in the first person, each one in a separate chapter, in Ann M. Martin's *Ten Kids, No Pets.*

SIMILE AND METAPHOR

Simile is an explicit comparison between two people, objects, or ideas, as in, "She looked like 'X'. . ." A more complex literary technique is the use of metaphor, a word or phrase denoting an idea in place of another to suggest a likeness or an analogy. Both permit readers to make inferences about story characters, finding the "missing connection" between what is written in the text and the readers' knowledge of the world. Using them, readers can interpret characters' personalities based on the author's clues.

Felice Homan uses metaphor in *Slake's Limbo* to subtly reveal the change in Slake's character by writing:

> It might be said of Slake that he had spent all of his life on the underside of the stones. For the first time now he became sharply aware that he was walking *on* not under.

As readers explore authors' individual styles they will become increasingly aware of how characters are crafted through words. Students need opportunity to share their insights in book talks before they practise this craft in their own writing, so it is appropriate for developing rather than beginning writers. (See the section on "Word Collector's Chair" in "Reading".)

For Developing Writers: Similes and metaphors are generally used more in novels than in picture books. Exposure to well-developed story characters who are revealed through metaphor, such as Gilly in Katherine Paterson's *The Great Gilly Hopkins* or Lois Lowry's Anastasia Krupnik from *Anastasia Has the Answers*, will help readers experience how playing with words and images enriches an author's writing, and therefore a reader's understanding. Norton Juster's *As: A Surfeit of Similes* can be shared to point out the power of similes for older learners.

EXPRESSION

Expressive writing tells others about one's personal feelings, experiences, or point of view. Because it is subjective and need not be written for an audience other than the writer, beginning writers often feel most comfortable with it. You can experiment with any of the following forms.

Autobiographies

For our purposes, autobiographies are life stories written in a chronological sequence from a first-person point of view. Many students often experience difficulty with this form as they want to include their entire life stories in one piece. Too often the text becomes a listing of facts rather than a description of memorable experiences. Sharing books like Christina Bjork's fictional autobiography of a young girl's trip to Paris, *Linnea in Monet's Garden*, may help students focus on an interesting episode in their own experience.

Kindergarten students can begin writing autobiographies with "All about Me" drawings and dictated stories. Beginning writers can organize important factual events in a narrative timeline using Susan Ramsey Hoguet's pictorial biography, *Solomon Grundy*, or Tomie de Paola's *The Art Lesson* as models. Older students can make an inventory of personal experiences and choose milestones in their lives to include in story-like texts entitled "Memories to Share".

You may want to start with oral sharing by getting students to collect a few objects that symbolize important personal events and display them on a clothesline. The students can then use the objects to briefly tell how these events relate to their lives.

teddy bear   plane ticket   drawing   newspaper clipping

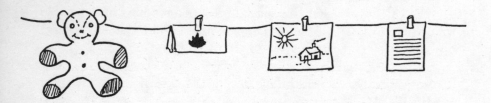

Because a full autobiography is an ambitious exercise for any of us, you may just want to have students collect their favorite stories about their experiences.

For Beginning Writers: Canadian painter William Kurelek highlights events from his life on the prairies in two beautifully illustrated picture books, *Prairie Boy's Summer* and *Prairie Boy's Winter*. Another painter, folk-artist Mattie Lou O'Kelley, describes her life growing up in the southern United States in *From the Hills of Georgia: An Autobiography in Paintings*. Vera Williams's adventure story, *Three Days on a River in a Red Canoe*, is fiction but told from a first-person point of view. Young writers can create picture books to describe specific events in their lives with brief texts written by them or dictated to proficient writers.

For Developing Writers: There are some excellent autobiographical models which older readers can use as inspirations for their own work. Jean Fritz's *Homesick: My Own Story* is based on facts recalled from the author's childhood, and her *China Homecoming* is her return to the country of her youth. Elizabeth Yates's *My Diary — My World* is an autobiography recorded in diary form. Lisl Weil's *I, Christopher Columbus* and Kathy Reynolds's *Marco Polo* are biographies, but they use first-person narratives which simulate the form of autobiography. Other interesting approaches are Brett Harvey's *My Prairie Year*, which is her grandmothers's diary reshaped into a story experience, or Peter Parnall's first-person account of the natural world in *Quiet*.

Learning Logs

Students can use learning logs to react to what they are learning in any subject of the curriculum. Writing is, after all, a valuable tool for learning in math, science, and social studies as well as language. Young writers can use these logs to reflect on emerging ideas, to explore ways of recording ideas, and to evaluate their own learning. There is no need to introduce students to models of literary logs in this activity, although you may encourage them to exchange their feelings as they write them down.

Jason, grade three, kept a learning log as he researched a report on fishing. His log reveals the struggles he had with the process and what he learned when he finished. Included are the teacher's comments as she responds to and supports Jason throughout the research process. These comments are really written conversations.

March 5th:

Today was the pits. I did not get anything down on my page because all there is are fish books and there is nothing in those about fishing.

[Teacher: Researching a topic is looking — not just writing.

I thought you worked very hard today and got lots done —
even if you didn't write.]

March 7th:

Today went terrific. I got some information on rods and
tomorrow I am going to write about fly fishing.

[Teacher: Sounds great — keep digging for information. P.S.
I have a book for you.]

March 11th:

Today went perfect. I looked for some stuff and found what
I was looking for and I have a strong feeling that I'm going
to have a few more excellent days. I have some stuff to write
about tomorrow.

[Teacher: You have a lot to write about!! Trust yourself —
you understand a lot about fishing and have some good
stories from your experiences. Include those in your
research.]

March 19th:

Today went terrific. I started to edit my work. I started to
understand that you do not start writing from your book
line by line. You pick out stuff you like and you put it in
your own little story.

[Teacher: I'm happy that you understand about writing the
story in your own words about what *you* know and *you*
learned. Today was a good day. Your story will be super.]

You can encourage your students to write about their reading
experiences in order to understand their own perceptions, to discover gaps in their knowledge, and to explore relationships
between what they are learning and their prior experiences. As
with learning logs, this writing should be used for expressing feelings and problem-solving rather than merely recording or regur-
gitating someone else's ideas.

In response to Katherine Paterson's *Bridge to Terabithia*, two
writers demonstrate their emotional reactions:

I felt like the book was not right. I mean it was not right to have Leslie die. At the beginning I sort of felt confused and frustrated. Why did a beautiful, wonderful, incredibly smart girl like Leslie have to die right after making everything right? I wish that it was all the dream that Jess had. It doesn't seem fair!!!

Nicole

At the beginning of when Terabithia was first started, I mean first built, I did not feel as if it was magic. But, when we got to the end I know it just had to be magic. When the book ended I felt sad, and my eyes were watering. I really liked the last sentence. It made me feel much better, because it sort of took over the sadness.

Caroline

Another writer discusses the writer's craft:

I liked the ending because the author stopped somewhere where you wanted to read on. In her next book, I hope she starts right where she left off! It made me feel like I was the one with the secret fort, TERABITHIA.

Brent

You can take this sort of writing further by encouraging students to respond to ideas in stories by connecting these to life experiences or trying to simulate the emotions and experiences of story characters.

For Beginning Writers: Younger students can relate the theme of a story to their personal lives. Disobeying a parent can be shared from a student's point of view after reading Beatrix Potter's *The Tale of Peter Rabbit*, Judith Viorst's *The Good-Bye Book*, or Jan Andrews's *Very Last First Time*.

For Developing Writers: Older students can assume the role of a story character and write a simulated learning log from that character's point of view. Orphaned Elspeth Macdonald, a Scottish girl who faces difficulties as she immigrates to western Canada with her little brother in Margaret Anderson's *The Journey* *of the Shadow Bairns*; Sweetgrass, the young Blackfoot girl who faces a threatening smallpox epidemic in Jan Hudson's *Sweetgrass*; Dicey Tillerman, who tries to keep her family together in Cynthia Voight's *Dicey's Song*; Mike Rankin, who comes to understand the meaning of life as he faces his own death in Monica Hughes's *Hunter in the Dark*; or Harriet, who keeps a notebook of her observations in Louise Fitzhugh's *Harriet the Spy*, are all story characters who could write log entries reflecting on their experiences.

Letters to the Editor

This form permits students to state an opinion based on a strong belief about a topic of interest, real or imaginary, that may be controversial or of personal concern. To provide practice in writing about a personal opinion, suggest that students write a letter to an editor in defense of a book character's actions.

For Beginning Writers: Younger students can defend the actions of the dog in Jenny Wagner's *John Brown, Rose and the Midnight Cat*, or the advice given by the rabbi in Margot Zemach's *It Could Always Be Worse*.

For Developing Writers: Older students can comment about the independence and resourcefulness of Claudia Kincaid as she runs away from home and lives in comfort in E.L. Konigsburg's *From the Mixed-up Files of Mrs. Basil E. Frankweiler*, the personal decision of Isobel Macpherson to return to her native heritage in Brenda Bellingham's *Storm Child*, the insistence of Queenie in Robert Burch's *Queenie Peavy* that she will be a doctor someday, not a nurse, the consequences of Joel's choice in Marion Dane Bauer's *On My Honor*, or Fran Ellen's disappointment in her little sister's return to a foster home in *Fran Ellen's House*.

Letters to Story Characters

One of the best ways to help students understand character development is to thrust them into the lives of actual story characters. By writing letters to such characters, students can become characters themselves, part of the story, as they record their personal views and feelings. They can write about actual situations in a story or create imaginary ones.

For Beginning Writers: Phillippe Dupasquier's *Dear Daddy* consists of Sophie's letters to her father, who is away on a cargo ship. Her letters describe her family life while Daddy is away. Janet and Allen Ahlberg's *The Jolly Postman* provides humorous letters to well-known story characters. The letters are in a variety of formats to open up and read: invitation, flyer, complaint, apology, business letter, birthday card, and postcard. After you share and discuss the book with your students, they will want to write their own letters to their favorite story characters about topics of interest.

For Developing Writers: Beverly Cleary's *Dear Mr. Henshaw* consists mostly of letters from a young boy, Leigh Botts, to his favorite author, Mr. Henshaw. The letters reveal the boy's anxieties as he struggles to overcome family problems. Students can respond by writing letters of support to Leigh. Other models include Elizabeth Borcher's *Dear Sarah*. Sarah's father writes to her during his travels to European cities. Students could write to Sarah describing their city, write to historical figures in literature to tell them what the world is like today, describing whatever interests them — space exploration, new technology, the Olympics, etc.

Advice Columns

In this activity, students respond to simulated problems that story characters raise in letters to a newspaper advice columnist. This is still expressive writing — the students' opinions should be their own — but remind them that their advice will have consequences for any characters who follow it.

For Beginning Writers: Encourage students to identify an episode in their favorite folktale that caused a story character unhappiness or concern and to write advice to that character. Students can write to Tomie de Paola's *Fin M'Coul: The Giant of Knockmany Hill* about ways to outwit the giant, or to Gerald McDermott's *Daniel O'Rourke* about staying out of trouble.

For Developing Writers: Following research on outdoor survival, older students can advise Karana in Scott O'Dell's *Island of the Blue Dolphins* about ways to survive alone on a deserted island, Lance in Marilyn Halvorson's *Nobody Said It Would Be Easy* about surviving in the wilderness after a plane crash, Gary

Paulsen's Brian in *Hatchet* about surviving fifty-four days alone in the Canadian wilderness, or Penuik in James Houston's *Wolf Run* about surviving in the Canadian Arctic, in a Ranger Rick Column.

Narration

Narrative writing tells a story, either true or fictional. All stories have characters, settings, and plots, but these vary in importance, depending on the purposes and styles of their authors. By the time students have begun to write brief sketches or stories about their own lives, they have also begun to understand the dazzling variety of possibilities for stories. They can be funny or sad, mysterious, fantastic, action-packed or quiet.

"Realistic" stories may be the simplest ones for many students to write because they are most like the students' own experiences, but they should be encouraged to try different forms. Some of the most common ones follow, but first some advice about getting writers started on stories, no matter what kind.

Story Beginnings

Existing literature is not only an excellent stimulus for writing, it also provides models for beginning a piece of writing. Observing the way an author begins a story will provide students with some alternatives to the "Once upon a time. . ." beginning that is typical of emergent writers. The discussion of many literary models through shared reading, book talks, and Word Collector's Chair (see "Reading") will help build a sense of "story leads".

For Beginning Writers: A short mini-lesson illustrated with many examples can show beginning writers how authors use a variety of techniques to lead readers into a piece.

For instance, Robert San Souci begins *The Talking Eggs*, a Creole folktale, by introducing readers to the characters:

> Back in the old days there was a widow with two daughters named Rose and Blanche.

Cherry Denman begins *The Little Peacock's Gift* by describing the setting:

It was midsummer in the forest and the air was hot and heavy.

For Developing Writers: Older writers need many models so they can refine an existing piece of writing. By reading aloud and discussing some of the strategies authors use to capture readers' interest, students will become aware of them in their own free reading.

Theodora Kroeber begins *Ishi Last of His Tribe* by using the setting to create a mood:

> Morning mists, white and still, filled Yuna Canyon, clinging to boulders and bushes, and to the round, earth-covered houses in the village of Tuliyani.

Ann Gabhart introduces readers to the action in *The Gifting* with:

> I sat in the back of the car, trying to act calm, while I strained for my first glimpse of the new house.

And Scott O'Dell explains the faraway setting in *Zia*, the sequel to *Island of the Blue Dolphins*:

> After one of the big storms that come in from the islands, our shore is covered with small clams.

Once readers have explored such different beginnings, they should feel more comfortable about starting their own stories.

Legends

Legends are stories handed down orally. Although fictional, they are generally based on some truth. Either a hero or heroine did live, or certain events did take place, but storytellers have stretched and exaggerated them in order to make them more interesting.

Students can write legends about incidents or characters from social studies or science themes. They might start by telling each other stories before they sit down to write.

For Beginning Writers: You may wish to have younger students try writing a legend about a geographical name or location. The name of your particular city or locale could generate an interesting story. Some literary models would be Jeanne M. Lee's *Legend of the Milky Way* and *The Legend of Li River*, or Linda Wason-Ellam's *The Legend of Calgary*. An alternative would be to have students write a legend about a holiday or Christmas character using Charles Mikolaycak's *Babushka*, Tomie de Paola's *The Legend of Old Befana*, or Ezra Jack Keats's *Little Drummer Boy* as models.

For Developing Writers: Older students can craft an original story about a legendary character by embroidering brave deeds. After sharing the adventure and noble deeds in Margaret Hodges's *Saint George and the Dragon*, Bernard Miles's *Robin Hood: His Life and Legend*, James Riordan's *Tales of King Arthur*, Selina Hastings's *Sir Gawain and the Loathly Lady*, Neil Philip's *The Tale of Sir Gawain*, or Ruth Robinson's *Taliesan and King Arthur*, ask students to write their own stories set in similar places and times. This activity requires students to have some knowledge of medieval times and may be done after they have researched a topic of interet. Mitsumasa Anno's *Medieval World*; John Goodall's wordless book, *Above and Below Stairs*, and Sheila Sancha's *The Luttrell Village: Country Life in the Middle Ages* will all help build medieval background for students.

Myths

Myths are stories created to explain the origin of the world and other natural phenomena, but unlike legends (which, however, they are often called), myths generally incorporate supernatural elements.

Native Americans and Canadians and the Inuit have developed a rich heritage of myths and legends which are still passed on orally by tribal storytellers. Some of these stories are being written down and used in teaching multicultural literature, as you will see below.

For Beginning Writers: Share richly illustrated single tales of North American myths with younger writers: Elizabeth Cleaver's *The Enchanted Caribou*, Paul Goble's *The Girl Who Loved Wild*

Horses and *Star Boy*, Murdo Scribe's *Murdo's Story*, Tomie de Paola's *The Legend of the Indian Paintbrush*, William Toye's *The Loon's Necklace* and *The Mountain Goats of Temlaham*, and John Steptoe's *The Story of Jumping Mouse*. Then have the students write their own myths.

For Developing Writers: Share Christie Harris's *Mouse Woman and the Vanished Princess*, Byrd Baylor's *Moon Song*, Muriel Whittaker's *Tales of the Canadian North*, and Robert San Souci's *The Legend of Scarface* before students write their own myths. This is what Heidi, a girl in grade four, wrote after reading *How the Sun Made a Promise and Kept It*, by Margery Bernstein and Janet Korbin, in which a beaver figures prominently.

How the Beaver Got Its Tail

Heidi

Long, long ago, when beavers had long, skinny tails, it was a bright, sunny day. Mr. Beaver told Mrs. Beaver that he was going out to chop down wood to build a new dam. Mr. Beaver put on a pair of old trousers and his rubber boots.

"I'll be back in an hour," Mr. Beaver told Mrs. Beaver. Mr. Beaver waved good-bye and set out in the woods. On his way he met up with one of his Beaver friends Charlie.

"Hey, Mr. Beaver," shouted Charlie, "over here." Mr. Beaver wobbled over to Charlie and found out that Charlie was chopping down wood too. They walked together deeper and deeper into the woods until they came to five or six huge maple trees.

"Let's start chopping down wood now. Before it gets dark," said Mr. Beaver. Charlie decided that that was a good idea. Charlie started sawing down the tree with his big, buck teeth. Charlie shouted timber and the tree went crashing down. Right on Mr. Beaver's tail! Mr. Beaver cried with pain.

"Gee Mr. Beaver, I'm really sorry," whispered Charlie guiltily.

"O.K.," said Mr. Beaver, "just get this tree off of me." Without another word Charlie tugged at the tree. Soon the tree rolled off and Mr. Beaver stared at his tail. Both of the beavers just stared at each other and laughed. Mr. Beaver's tail was totally flat. So that's how the beaver got its tail.

Tall Tales

Tall tales are adventure stories peppered with a mixture of boastful humor, bravado, and pioneer spirit. Tall tale characters are known for their exaggerated size and strength — and their claims of outfighting, outrunning, and outbragging just about everyone. Paul Bunyan, the North Woods lumberman, and Pecos Bill, the Texas cowboy, are both tall tale heroes. Not to be outmatched is Joe Mufferaw, a Canadian giant lumberjack from the Ottawa Valley. Exposure to stories featuring such characters will help students stretch their imaginations to write about their own make-believe characters who can perform impossible feats.

For Beginning Writers: Sharing Ariane Dewey's *Pecos Bill* and *Febold Feboldson*, Glen Rounds's Paul Bunyan in *The Morning the Sun Refused to Shine*, Caron Lee Cohen's *Sally Ann Thunder Ann Whirlwind Crockett*, Steven Kellogg's *Paul Bunyan* and *Johnny Appleseed: A Tall Tale* with younger students will acquaint them with tall tale characters and their humorous antics. They might create puppets of tall tale characters before writing their own stories.

For Developing Writers: The descriptive language patterns loaded with comparatives ("-ers") and superlatives ("-ests") can be developed for older students in Jim Aylesworth's *Shenandoah Noah*, Trinka Hakes Noble's *Meanwhile Back at the Ranch*, Bernie Bedore's *Tall Tales of Joe Mufferaw*, and Virginia Haviland's *North American Legends*. Students can model the tall tale humor in James Stevenson's *We Hate Rain* when Grandfather reminisces about his boyhood, the roguish adventure of Jean Lafitte in Ariane Dewey's *Lafitte the Pirate*, or the fresh twist in the story of Noah and his Ark in Glen Rounds's *Washday on Noah's Ark*. They may want to write collectively a Big Book of tall tales about their favorite character.

Trickster Tales

Many characters, animal or human, in folk literature trick and outwit their adversaries through their cleverness. Every culture throughout the world has its own trickster tales, conflicts between a clever character and a foolish one. Such conflicts between characters bring excitement to tales and help move plots forward.

Many African tales are about animal tricksters such as Anansi the spider, Zomo the rabbit, and Ijapa the tortoise. Animal trickster tales are also popular throughout North America; their protagonists are often coyotes, rabbits, or ravens who use transformations in their clever pranks. Brer Rabbit and Raven are both well-known tricksters in American folklore.

After reading and discussing a variety of trickster tales to see how authors develop conflicts between trickster characters who cunningly outwit others, students can select animals to develop as tricksters in their own tales.

For Beginning Writers: Younger readers can enjoy the fox as a trickster in a number of tales: Isabel Barclay's *Fox and Bear*, and Paul Galdone's *The Gingerbread Boy, Henny Penny*, and *Three Aesop Fox Fables*. For contrast present the reverse plot: the predator fox outwitted by a clever child in Pat McKissack's *Flossie and the Fox*, by a mouse dentist in William Steig's *Doctor DeSoto*, by a cow in Mem Fox's *Hattie and the Fox*, by an old woman in Paul Galdone's *What's in Fox's Sack?* or Jennifer Westwood's *Going to Squintum's: A Foxy Folktale*, and by a hen in Pat Hutchins's *Rosie's Walk*, Barbara Cooney's *Chanticleer and the Fox*, and Margaret Berrill's *Chanticleer*.

For Developing Writers: Gail Robinson's *Raven, the Trickster: Legends of the North American Indians*, Beth Ahenakew and Sam Hardlotte's *Story of Wesakechak*, Christie Harris's *Mouse Woman and the Mischief-Makers*, Emerson and David Coatsworth's *The Adventures of Nanabush*, Linda Pelly's *Saulteaux Legends* (Nanabush), and John Bierhorst's *Doctor Coyote: A Native American Aesop's Fables* are excellent collections. Students can be stretched with Marcia Brown's *Shadow*, a highly illustrated poem that uses metaphor to suggest that shadows are tricksters. They can also trace and compare variations of trickster characters across cultures: Anansi in Jamaican folktales from Phillip Sherlock's *Anansi the Spider Man* versus the West African tales in Joyce Cooper Arhurst's *The Adventures of Spider*; Hugh Sturton's Zomo in *Zomo the Rabbit* versus Iktomi, the rabbit from North American folklore, in Paul Goble's *Iktomi and the Berries* and *Iktomi and the Boulder*, versus Brer Rabbit from Julius Lester's *The Tales of Uncle Remus* or Jacqueline Schachter Weiss's *Young Brer Rabbit and Other Trickster Tales from the Americas*.

More human trickster characters include the leprechaun in Elizabeth Schute's *Clever Tom and the Leprechaun: An Old Irish Story*, Taro in Dianne Snyder's *The Boy of the Three Year Nap*, and Aladdin in Marianne Mayer's *Aladdin and the Enchanted Lamp*.

Mysteries

Mysteries are adventure stories with problems to solve through puzzle clues. A good mystery keeps a reader in suspense until the climax, when an unexpected relationship between events or characters usually solves the riddle. Mysteries stimulate critical thinking by encouraging readers and writers to make inferences in order to arrive at solutions.

The plots of most mysteries should be carefully planned. Before they write their own, students need to read mysteries and examine their characteristics by recording their ideas on a chart like the following:

MYSTERIES

- Have problems (crimes) to solve

- Main characters work to solve these problems (crimes)

- The plot develops as clues are introduced

- Some clues are relevant and lead to solving the problem (crime)

- Other clues are not relevant and lead the problem-solver (detective) astray

---

For Beginning Writers: Younger students can practise solving mysteries by looking for clues in Steven Kellogg's *The Mystery of the Magic Green Ball* and *The Mystery of the Missing Red Mitten*, Verna Aardema's *Who's In Rabbit's House?*, Ruth Brown's *A Dark, Dark Tale*, James Stevenson's *What's under My Bed?*, and Tony Ross's *I'm Coming to Get You*. Fernando Krahn's wordless book *The Mystery of Giant Footprints* invites students to create their own text.

For Developing Writers: More complex mysteries with interwoven clues include Ellen Raskin's *The Westing Game* and *The*

Mysterious Disappearance of Leon (I Mean Noel), both of which provide experience in solving word puzzles. Rumer Godden's *The Rocking Horse Secret*, Georges McHargue's *Funny Bananas*, Philippa Pearce's *The Way to Sattin Shore*, C.S. Adler's *Footsteps on the Stairs*, and Beverly Butler's *Ghost Cat* are suspense-filled tales. Avi's *Who Stole the Wizard of Oz?* draws composite clues for students who have previously read *The Wind in the Willows*, *Through the Looking Glass*, *Treasure Island*, and *Winnie-the-Pooh*. Chris Van Allsburg's almost wordless picture book *The Mysteries of Harris Burdick* challenges students to create stories for the text.

Poetry

Poetry is a natural form of expression for many young writers. It helps them explore feelings and ideas by playing with language and rhythm or rhyme to create word pictures, vivid images, and multi-sensory comparisons.

The range of possibilities in poetry is perhaps wider than in any other form: it can be expressive or narrative, rhyme or free verse. But it should be approached with care. Students must listen to a lot of poetry and experiment with word play, especially metaphor, before they create their own poems. Some poetic forms (such as rigid rhyming schemes) force structure too soon. Students should be free to use their natural language patterns in free verse rather than sacrifice their ideas in order to achieve a rhyming pattern. Non-rhyming structures that feature a rhythmic formula can lead to successful poetry writing. Such rhythmic arrangements give students a structure in which to organize their ideas without paralysing them with strict rules. The poetry activities in this book focus on non-rhyming structures, because they encourage play: you may want to explore verse on your own.

Free Verse

Free verse is characterized by a lack of rhyme and fairly unpredictable rhythm. Arnold Adoff's poems about athletes in *Sports Pages*, Myra Cohn Livingston's figurative language in *Sky Songs*, the rhythmic chants of Byrd Baylor's *Desert Voices*, and the imagery of Cynthia Rylant's autobiographical poems in *Waiting to Waltz, A Childhood* provide some excellent literary models.

Students can use free verse to react to a character or a theme from a story. Free verse often paints a word picture, as in this grade four student's tribute to Searchlight, the dog in John Gardiner's *Stone Fox*:

> Searchlight
> You were there for me
> When I needed you.
> Best friend
>
> Kevin

Shape

Shape poetry is a whimsical form that makes a visual picture as well as a verbal statement. It is sometimes called "concrete poetry". Robert Froman's *Seeing Things* and *Street Poems* can be used as literary models. In response to Dalia Hardof Renberg's *Hello, Clouds!*, a grade four student responded:

Lili

Cinquains

A cinquain is a non-rhyming shape poem composed of five lines, each with a special purpose. Students can have fun playing with words and arranging them into a cinquain. A writing assignment could be built around taking thoughts about a story character and translating them into a cinquain. A simple form of the cin-quain could include:

Line 1: Subject .... 1 word
Line 2: Description of the subject .... 2 words
Line 3: Action about the subject .... 3 words
Line 4: Feeling about the subject .... 3 words
Line 5: Synonym for the subject .... 1 word

Well-developed story characters work for this type of poetry, as in this example by Jessica, grade four, suggested by Miska Miles's *Annie and the Old One:*

Annie
loving, young
Holding back time
unaccepting, wishing, frightened
grand-daughter

For Beginning Writers: Share Ivan Sherman's *Walking Talking Words* with beginners to show how shapes can stretch the imagination.

For Developing Writers: Older writers can enjoy Barbara Juster Ebensen's *Words with Wrinkled Knees: Animal Poems* or Arnold Adoff's *Birds,* in which words are skillfully arranged on the page to visually complement the sounds of the language. Students can integrate art and poetry by exploring a number of art activities that could extend or embellish their poems (see "Art").

Exposition

Expository writing informs and explains. It is the language of science, academia, and news, and it requires as much objectivity as possible on the part of the writer. Just as students can start writing fiction by drawing brief character or episodic sketches, so in non-fiction they can start with brief accounts of events.

Eye Witness News Reports

Eye witness news stories generally give information about interesting people and events in short, factual reports from the point of view of an objective observer. Good news stories inform by answering the "W + H" questions: Who, What, Where, When, Why, and How.

They can take a variety of forms, from radio or television broadcasts to newspaper or magazine articles.

Since many stories have exciting and action-filled plots, students can first listen to a story and then assume the role of a news reporter and write an eye witness news report about the story. Picture books with shorter, simpler plots are better for encouraging this type of writing activity than longer fiction. To start, you might ask students to write a collaborative news report and then deliver it to the class, playing the roles of news reporters.

For Beginning Writers: Mira Lobe's *The Snowman Who Went for a Walk*, Trinka Hakes Nobles's *The Day Jimmy's Boa Ate the Wash*, John Burningham's *John Patrick Norman McHennessy — The Boy Who Was Always Late*, Molly Bang's *Tye May and the Magic Brush*, and Stephen Gammell's *Once upon MacDonald's Farm* are humorous fantasies that can be retold as news reports. Students can also retell wordless picture books with well-developed plots, such as Brinton Turkel's *Deep in the Forest* and Tomie de Paola's *The Hunter and the Animals*. (A full list of useful wordless picture books and their plots appears in the bibliography for this chapter at the end of the book.)

For Developing Writers: David Macaulay's *Why the Chicken Crossed the Road* and Colin West's *The King of Kennelwick Castle*, both stories with chain reaction plots, or Arnold Adoff's cumulative poem *The Cabbages Are Chasing the Rabbits* and Jay Willams's *Everyone Knows What a Dragon Looks Like* work well with older writers.

Any exciting adventure story can be rewritten as an eye witness news report. Students can either use a chapter or summarize the entire story. Vesper Holly's quests for traces of a lost kingdom in Lloyd Alexander's *The Illyrian Adventures*, and Matthew and Kayak's rescue in James Houston's *Frozen Fire* or their search for gold in *Black Diamonds* make interesting news stories.

Research Reports

Once students have learned to write brief news reports, they can go on to more complex ones. Report writing offers them opportunities to research a chosen topic in a content area of study and to write creatively about it, organizing and presenting facts, generalizations, and opinions. They can gather information from a variety of print and non-print sources such as magazines, reference books, newspapers, atlases, almanacs, films, television, and even interviews they conduct themselves. They will need instruction and guidance in learning how to find, prepare, and present their material.

There are six basic steps in report writing, and they are each dealt with here.

1. Choose a Topic

There are several ways to help students choose topics. Some teachers prefer to select a class theme for all students that relates to a content area and then let each student select a topic within that theme. Others prefer to let students choose their own topics, usually related to their hobbies or personal interests. The latter approach enables students to research answers to their own questions, and that helps motivate them.

An example of a self-chosen topic is *The History and Facts of Business* by Jeannie, a student in grade three. She chose this subject because of a personal interest which she explains in a response to the question, "How did you choose your topic?"

BUSINESS

One evening the phone rang. It was my dad. He started to talk about a new job. When my mom got off the phone she was a bit excited. She said . . . your dad might be opening his own business. A man will loan him the money and help him get started. I was very excited. I was even jumping on furniture. When my mom told me about this business I got extremely interested in what my dad was doing. My dad and I get along terrifically well and what concerns me concerns him and what concerns him concerns me. What he is doing is important to me and this is why I am interested in business.

71

2. Brainstorm

The purpose of brainstorming is to activate prior knowledge so students can retrieve information that they already know or think they know about a topic, and try to figure out what else they want to discover about it.

Jeannie began her brainstorming by listing information she already knew about business and information she wanted to research.

WHAT I KNEW

I knew you needed equipment,
advertisement, trading, employees,
training skill, and that is all I knew
before starting research [into] why start
a business.

WHAT I WANTED TO KNOW

How to start one
How you decide to start one
How to get employees
How business began
Why start one
What is a résumé

3. Gather Information

Students need guidance in where to locate information, how to take notes by paraphrasing information (jotting down key words or phrases rather than copying sentences), and how to keep track of information. Teacher-librarians can assist students with the initial instruction in these skills by first guiding small groups of students through the collaborative writing of a class report. First, orientation to resources such as card catalogues, tables of contents, indexes, etc. are given to those students who have limited experience in locating information. Then students gain practice in note-taking by first silently reading a piece of text presented on an overhead transparency while the teacher-librarian reads it orally. Next the transparency is removed and students record

the main idea and the important details by clustering the information on a chart. Clustering is a strategy similar to brainstorming, except that ideas are circled and linked to the main idea in
a web-like diagram. Clustering gives students opportunity to summarize information and separate a main idea from the details
without copying directly from the reference. Finally, students
can write a brief paragraph using their own words to organize,
order, and relate these ideas.

Jeannie made the following diagram:

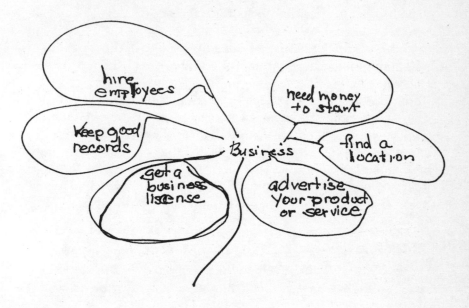

Jeannie listed the resources she used for writing her report:

SOURCES

The Principles of Modern Management (a book)
Mr. Burt
Mrs. Horning   interviews
Mr. Ryan
Honest Business (a book)

Throughout the research process, Jeannie kept a learning log that gave insight into how she was doing her research. This reflective writing became a "window" onto the research process. Jeannie's struggles with the process of finding a focus is evident in the following entry:

3-05-87

I am starting to understand . . . what I really want to talk about and what I want to know . . . finding information is easy but trying to see my question in the book isn't.

Her teacher responded to Jeannie in the journal:

. . . finding answers to your questions is one of the most difficult things about research. But it will probably be worth it.

Interviewing deserves special attention and instruction. When interviewing, students must learn to get others to talk about what they know and to keep track of what they say so that the information learned can be put in writing. They need practice in drafting open-ended questions that elicit facts, opinions, or feelings.

Jeannie interviewed people in her community who had expertise in business. She commented about some of them in her log:

3-12-87

Today when I interviewed Mrs. Horning I found something which was really neat. When I asked her a question she said the same answer as a book and a man so I knew it was important.

4. Select a Format

Once they have done their research, students need to review it and consider a point of view and a format for sharing it. There are numerous innovative literary models for presenting material combining print and graphics in such a way that they add interest and visual appeal for the reader. Traditional formats are being augmented to include fold-outs, pop-ups, overlays, cut-away pages and lift-a-flap construction that create three-dimensional effects. Other suggestions for presenting research reports include question and answer books, slide-tapes, and filmstrip presentations.

5. Organize Information

The most common way of organizing content in expository writing is to present ideas in a hierarchical relationship, introducing the most important ideas at the beginning of the text and subordinate ideas later. Students may find it helpful to number their notes in the order in which they plan to use them. Any charts, diagrams, maps, pictures, or timelines should be included in the planning.

Jeannie organized her report in a Big Book by responding to each of her research questions on a separate page using a question and answer format.

HOW BUSINESS FIRST BEGAN?

Business started over eight thousand years ago. The first business people were actually traders. Their ways were even carried over to cities in later time. It first started out as a bartering system. First people would trade things and after a while a wise man had an idea. He thought that people should dig for gold and silver so they did and later on their backs were hurting so they made paper money and we still trade today. We trade money for goods.

6. Publish

In publishing a research report, students should use the process approach to writing by drafting, editing, and revising. When the final report is polished, then it is time to assemble the text and all other elements, such as illustrations, table of contents, cover, title page, and bibliography. (See "Art" for information about making books.) Here is what Jeannie's final report looked like (note that although Jeannie is female and actually interviewed a businesswoman, the figures on the cover of her report are all male; you could point this out in your response to the report):

Business

WHY DO YOU WANT TO START A BUSINESS

— Be your own boss.
— I want to make lots of money for myself and family not for some large corporation.
— I want to be in this town. I don't want to be transferred.
— I want to decide how hard I'll work and when I'll work.
— I don't want to go to school anymore.
— I want to work for myself.

HOW TO GET EMPLOYEES

The most popular and efficient way of getting employees is by advertising. Employers use the media and employment agencies.

In some instances an employer will train someone to do a certain job. This is what is referred to as an apprentice. This system is usually not as expensive as if a fully trained person was hired.

WHAT IS A RÉSUMÉ

The people that are going to get the job need a résumé. The résumé tells of what they did in college and where they have worked before, what experience they have and what *they know already* about the job. It helps the person who's doing the hiring to know if the person who is applying for the job can handle it.

HOW SOME PEOPLE DECIDE TO START ONE

Their friends encouraged them to. They said you should be your own boss. You can do it can't you. You will be the first one to start one in this job don't give up.

Another person said they were interested in the type of business it was and they wanted to be proud of themselves for what they just did.

Others said they had a big need to have their own business. They are tired of working for someone else and want to be independent and not dependent. When owning a business of your own a person feels that they can always operate it better than a previous employer.

WHAT ARE THE THINGS YOU START OFF WITH IN A BUSINESS

First thing to consider in starting a business is the marketability of the product to be sold or the service to be provided. The proper location is very important. For example a shoe store wouldn't do very well near a school but a candy store would. The next consideration would be the expenses for stock, rent, staff, utilities, overhead and unexpected expenses. You also need proper equipment. You need a license.

CONCLUSION

In this project I found it interesting, fun but hard. It took a lot of time and patience. I not only learned how to start and manage a business but also the history of business. In researching this project I met very interesting people.

Work on research reports can be integrated with reading for information and reading across the curriculum (see "Reading"). These reports should not simulate the "encyclopedia" style but reflect the current trend of literature in the content area: a picture book format with illustrations, pop-ups, or fold-outs. Many of the activities in the chapter on art can be used for bookmaking suggestions.

It should be remembered that research can be used for writing fiction, as students need a knowledge base before they can write about experiences that are not their own. They can, for instance, do historical research for stories set in the past. By the same token, reading fiction can sometimes suggest subjects for writing non-fiction, as noted below.

For Beginning Writers: Cynthia Rylant's *When I Was Young in the Mountains*, Betty Waterton's *Pettranella*, Barbara Brenner's *Wagon Wheels*, Ann Blades's *Mary of Mile 18*, Sue Ann Alderson's *Ida and the Wool Smugglers*, and Don Hall's *Oxcart Man* give young readers a suggestion of life in long-ago times.

For Developing Writers: Carol Ryrie Brink's *Caddie Woodlawn*, Harold Keith's *The Obstinate Land*, Anne Pelowksi's *Winding Valley Farm: Annie's Story*, Pam Conrad's *Prairie Songs*, and Laura

Ingalls Wilder's books give older readers an understanding of the physical environment from the viewpoint of several story characters.

Persuasion

Persuasive writing is a particular kind of expository writing intended to persuade an audience to accept a belief or opinion. Advertisements and editorials are both examples of persuasive writing.

Advertisements

These are a good way to start because most children are very familiar with advertisements intended to persuade people to buy either a service or a product. Ads provide a great exercise in combining words and pictures in a way that attracts attention. Students can write advertisements for their favorite books using language that highlights their best features and makes them appealing to other readers.

For Beginning Writers: Ideas for younger students might include writing an advertisement about the versatility of a particular animal. Shel Silverstein's *Who Wants a Cheap Rhinoceros?* is an excellent literary model using both words and pictures to enumerate a variety of practical uses for a rhinoceros. Silverstein anticipates and counters the reader's objections to his arguments for owning such a wonderful animal. A similar tale is Harry Allard's *It's So Nice to Have a Wolf around the House*. An alternate idea would be to write an advertisement to help Big Anthony from Tomie de Paola's *Strega Nona* get rid of all that spaghetti or to help the peddler in Esphyr Slobodkina's *Caps for Sale* sell all his caps.

For Developing Writers: Older writers can develop illustrated travel brochures to advertise special places found in books that might lure travellers. Katherine Paterson's *Bridge to Terabithia*, Lloyd Alexander's Land of Prydain in *The Book of Three*, Janet Lunn's *The Root Cellar*, and C.S. Lewis's *The Lion, the Witch and the Wardrobe* all contain fantasy settings to visit. A more challenging setting would be Monica Hughes's futuristic world in *The Dream Catcher*.

Editorials

Editorials require students to present an opinion or an attitude towards a news event or a topic of concern. Students must first develop a personal opinion about the topic and then write from that point of view. The exercise involves an objectivity that makes it more suitable for older students.

All children need opportunities to identify with their own cultural heritage and to appreciate the cultures of others. After reading about story characters who identify with their heritage, they can write an editorial on taking pride in one's heritage.

For Developing Writers: Discuss Cassie Logan's feelings for her black heritage in Mildred Taylor's *Roll of Thunder, Hear Me Cry*, Plum Langor's Indian roots in Evelyn Sibley Lampman's *Potlatch Family*, Shirley Temple Wong's bond with her Chinese culture in Betty Bao Lord's *In the Year of the Boar and Jackie Robinson*, or May and Lee's native heritage in Barbara Smucker's *White Mist* by exploring how these story characters' ideas may match or differ from students' feelings about their own culture.

All the kinds of writing described in this chapter encourage students to make meaning through language, but in the whole language classroom, writing is only one of a rich variety of ways to absorb and express meaning. We turn now to some of the others.

CHAPTER FIVE

Art

Art is a vital part of any whole language classroom because it gives students a wide choice of ways to express their thoughts and feelings. Sometimes they may understand an idea expressed through art that they might not have understood through words alone. Many whole language teachers use art activities both as a way to explore ideas before reading or writing and as a way to encourage students to reflect on their ideas after reading and writing.

Like writing, art is both a process and a product, but most traditional classrooms focus on it as a product. Too often teachers give students crayons and paper and ask them to draw a picture to accompany a story or poem without providing the background needed to make the learning experience successful. This chapter is intended to help you use different activities and strategies to enrich your students' experience of art.

Creating art forces students to think visually, to exercise their imaginations, and to perceive relationships between parts and wholes as they view and interpret the world. Learning in art is like learning in whole language. The process of making visual art engages students in converting materials into ideas, images, or feelings. There are three stages in the creation of art: generating ideas, making meaning, and extending ideas. Initially artists must plan and rehearse ideas about how to visually represent intended forms and shapes; later, they continually refine and rearrange during the process as problems arise and solutions are generated.

Marni, a grade three student, has written a research report on the cheetah, and now she wants to make it into a book.

Stage 1.
The artist builds background by generating ideas and exploring ways to express them visually.

I thought at first, I would use yellow and black felt markers to make the cheetah's fur and spots. Then I changed my mind when I realized the yellow might get smudged if I tried to shade it. So, I used paint to get the dark and light fur and felts for the spots.

GENERATING IDEAS

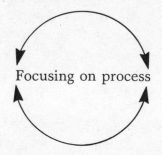

Focusing on process

Stage 2.
The artist makes meaning by designing, rearranging, and refining visual forms.

During the painting, Marni modified her strategies as she began to think of her picture as a whole rather than just focusing on the cheetah itself.

When I finished painting the cheetah, she looked okay. But

the background had a lot of empty spaces. So I used felt markers to color in the sky, some flowers and trees. I added two small cheetah cubs so the big one would not look so lonely.

MAKING MEANING

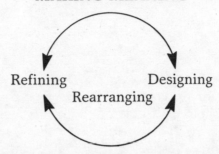

Refining   Designing
        Rearranging

Stage 3.
The artist extends ideas by exhibiting and sharing visual forms with others.

After completing her picture, Marni mounted it in a big book. But when she considered sharing it with others, she generated another story to express her visual interpretations.

After I finished my painting, I pasted it in my big book with the research report. When I looked at the picture, it looked like a mother cheetah with her cubs which didn't match what I said in my research report. So, I wrote another story about the cheetah family.

EXTENDING IDEAS

Reflecting on process

An effective art program introduces new forms to students while offering them instruction in both the elements of art and observational skills. Viewing different art styles in literary selections is an important aspect of learning as it sensitizes students to forms that they might not otherwise see and reinforces the idea that diversity and individuality in art are to be enjoyed and valued. Whole language teachers give their students a variety of media to choose from and provide ample time for experimentation.

Elements of Art

The elements of art can be taught in the classroom using a wide range of illustrations in children's picture books. Many picture books feature innovative graphic or three-dimensional techniques. Teachers can stimulate creativity in students by calling attention to the medium used by a particular illustrator and making appropriate art materials available for students to experiment with.

You can use books to help students observe and explore line, shape, texture, color, and form. But remember that the books should be merely a starting point for the students' own work, not examples that the students have to copy.

Gloria, grade three, explains a painting she made after looking at Brian Wildsmith's *Pelican*:

This is not a copy of Brian Wildsmith's picture but I used some of his technique to paint this picture. I used dark water-paint and collage. I used splatter painting and I used a tool to make texture on part of the picture that had thick paint on it.

Line

There are many kinds of lines that can be used to achieve different effects and communicate different feelings and ideas:

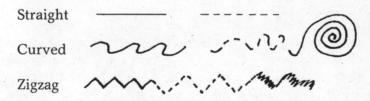

Lines can vary in direction:

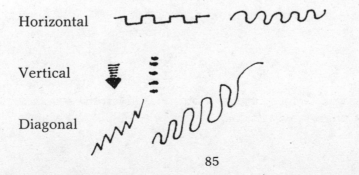

They can vary in width and length:

Thick   ▬▬▬▬

Thin   _____

Long   _____

Short   __ __ __

Expand your students' repertoire of lines by showing them the work of illustrators who use lines differently to suggest direction, movement, action, and mood.

For Beginning Artists: Students can observe and explore line as it creates details in Pat Hutchins's *The Surprise Party* and *One Hunter*, Paul Goble's *The Girl Who Loved Wild Horses*, and Robert Ravensky's intricate crosshatched lines in Richard Peveor's *Mister Cat-and-a-Half*.

For Developing Artists: Older students can appreciate how Shawn Steffler uses lines to form shapes in Don Gale's *Sooshewan: Child of the Beothuk*. Line can create intricate details as in Mitsumasa Anno's *Anno's Flea Market* and *Anno's Journey*, Heidi Holder's *Aesop's Fables*, Jan Brett's illustrations in Eve Bunting's *Scary, Scary Halloween*, and Chris Conover's *The Wizard's Daughter: A Viking Tale*.

Shape

A line that meets itself, or a block of color or texture, creates a shape:

Students can observe and explore how illustrators construct shapes in the following books.

For Beginning Artists: Shapes can be torn and arranged to create a picture as in Eric Carle's *The Very Quiet Cricket*, Leo Lionni's *Frederick*, and Elizabeth Cleaver's *The Mountain Goats of Temlaham*. Pat Hutchins uses shapes that change form in *Changes, Changes,* and Lois Ehlert uses cut-out shapes in *Color Zoo*.

For Developing Artists: Older students can look at overlapping shapes and observe how they can create depth as in Sheila White Samton's *Beside the Bay*. Gerald McDermott uses patterns of line and color to create shapes in *Arrow to the Sun* and *Anansi, the Spider*, while Ann Jonas's *Reflections* presents beach and forest scenes that become different images when viewed upside down.

Texture

Repeated lines create texture:

Repeated shapes create texture:

Students can observe and discuss how illustrators create textures, then apply different techniques to their own illustrations.

For Beginning Artists: Younger students can create texture through repeated lines or through crayon rubbings of several different surface textures. Leo Lionni's *Tico and the Golden Wings*, Tejima's lines and forms in *Ho-Limlim: A Rabbit Tale from Japan*, and Charles Mikolaycak's illustrations in *Babushka* all show texture.

For Developing Artists: Older students can experiment with color washes and a variety of instruments to create texture. Paul Goble's *Buffalo Woman*, Susan Jeffers's illustrations in Robert

Frost's *Stopping by Woods on a Snowy Evening*, Errol LeCain's illustrations in Henry Wadsworth Longfellow's *Hiawatha's Childhood* and *Aladdin and the Wonderful Lamp*, Ruth Robbins's in *Taliesin and King Arthur*, and Marilee Heyer's rich patterns in *The Weaving of a Dream* show different ways to create texture.

An interesting, sophisticated technique for creating texture is batik (a wax-resistant process), which Edda Reinl uses to illustrate *The Little Snake*, and Patricia MacCarthy prints on silk in *Animals Galore*.

Color

Color can create mood or express a feeling. Red, orange, and yellow are warm colors, while green, violet, and blue are cool. Overlapping colors create new colors.

Color can range from bright, vibrant hues to soft, shimmering radiances. It can be used to complement the mood, setting, characterization, and theme of a story. A nice way to introduce color is through Ruth Robbins's *How the First Rainbow Was Made*, an Indian legend about the creation of the rainbow, or through the mixing in Ann Jonas's *Color Dance* and Ellen Stohl Walsh's *Mouse Paint*.

For Beginning Artists: Younger students can observe the range of colors used by a variety of artists. Bold colors and strong images are created in Molly Bang's *Ten, Nine, Eight*, jewel-like colors in Brian Wildsmith's *Pelican*, and luminous colors in Lorinda Bryan Cauley's *Jack and the Beanstalk*. José Aruego and Ariane Dewey use acrylics to achieve vibrant colors in *We Hide, You Seek* and *One Duck Another Duck*. Marie Louise Gay uses scintillating color in the cartoon-like illustrations in *Moonbeam on a Cat's Ear*. Beatriz Vidal's multicolored pictures in Verna Aardema's *Bringing the Rain to Kapiti Plain* appear muted compared to the luminous colors of Barbara Berger's *Gwinna*.

For Developing Artists: Hilda Simon's *The Magic of Color* examines the world of color for older students. They can compare Ariane Dewey's dramatic color in *The Thunder God's Son*, Ed Young's soft watercolors in *Lon Po Po*, Michael Hague's dark, rich illustrations in Elizabeth Isele's *The Frog Princess* and *Aesop's Fables*, Ed Young's shimmering illustrations in Ruth Yaffe Radin's

High in the Mountains, and Lazlo Gal's soft-colored illustrations in Meghan Collins's *The Willow Maiden.*

Form

Illustrations need not appear two-dimensional. The illusions of perspective, shading, and lighting can all be used to create a three-dimensional look.

 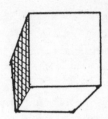

Forms can be organic, irregular, and curving, or geometric, rigid, and mechanical. Students should explore all kinds.

For Beginning Artists: Have students observe Barbara Reid's plasticine-relief illustrations in Joanne Oppenheim's *Have You Seen Birds?* and Edith Chase's *The New Baby Calf* or Mitsumasa Anno's visual illusions in *Anno's Alphabet.*

For Developing Artists: David Macaulay's illustrations in *Cathedral* give older students a sense of perspective within a cathedral. A similar technique is used in his other books, *City, Castle, and Pyramid.* Barbara Reid shares her technique for using plasticene as a modeling material in *Playing with Plasticine.*

Art Activities for Making Books

Making books is one of the best ways to share students' writing and give them a sense of pride in their work. A fascinating step-by-step method is detailed in Aliki's *How a Book Is Made.* Students need to see how books are made, the various media that can be used, the possible arrangements of words, the different designs of title pages, covers, and endpapers before they attempt their own. A wide range of art media and book-making techniques should be explored.

Once finished, books written and illustrated by students may be published and catalogued in the school library for sharing with other students. What follows is a brief survey of techniques your students can use to illustrate, design, and produce their own books.

Techniques for Illustration

Storyboarding

Storyboarding is a way of mapping out stories by illustrating key developments in their plots. It can be used by students to reflect on stories they have read or to help plan their own illustrated books.

In *The Sparrow's Song* by Ian Wallace, a brother and sister find an injured baby sparrow, nurse it back to health, and then — rather reluctantly — set it free. Here is what one student came up with to storyboard the plot in three illustrations depicting what happened first, what happened next, and what happened finally.

The Sparrow's Song

What happened first · What happened next · What happened finally

Remember that storyboards need not be polished work: they are intended to be rough thumbnail sketches of key events, a sort of road map for the flow of plot.

Older readers and writers can develop more elaborate storyboards consisting of much longer sequences of illustrations. The point should be to gain experience in analysing or planning plots without feeling pressured to produce "finished" works of art. Storyboarding is to art what a rough first or second draft is to writing. Once it is completed, students can sit down and work on the final art.

Painting

Students can blow, drip, spatter, sponge, spray, stencil, and/or scratch paint to create a variety of textual effects on dry, wet, or colored papers. Eric Carle spatters vibrant colors in *The Tiny Seed*, Keiko Narahashi's vivid and flowing shapes dominate the pages of *I Have a Friend*, James Stevenson streaks watercolor on the pages of Charlotte Zolotow's *Say It*, while Patricia MacCarthy paints batik on silk in Margaret Mahy's *17 Kings and 42 Elephants.*

To create a marble effect, artists can float blobs of acrylic paint on water, then lightly place a piece of paper over it. Nonny Hogrogian uses this technique for the endpapers and illustrations in the Grimm Brothers' tales, *The Glass Mountain* and *The Devil with the Three Golden Hairs.*

Scratchboard

Scratching dry black ink that has been painted over a shiny white surface produces crisp black and white illustrations. This technique is similar to crayon etching, in which bright colors are drawn or painted first on the paper, then a coat of a solid color of paint applied on top. When the surface is dry, a design can be scratched through to the color beneath.

Marcia Sewall's black and white scratchboard illustrations in Richard Kennedy's *Song of the Horse*, Robert Quakenbush's illustrations in Eleanor Clymer's *Horatio Goes to the Country*, and Barbara Cooney's illustrations for *Chanticleer and the Fox* are lovely models.

Collage

A collage is made by pasting different materials of different shapes and textures, or even bits of existing illustrations from magazines onto a surface to create a picture. Shapes can be torn or cut and then arranged to create texture. Painted or drawn sections can be combined with found materials to create a collage. Artists such as Eric Carle, Gerald McDermott, Ezra Jack Keats, Leo Lionni, and Elizabeth Cleaver use this technique in their books. Jeannie Baker creates three-dimensional, full-page collage illustrations in her story of a homing pigeon, *Home in the Sky*, Marcia Brown captures striking images in *Shadow*, and David Wisniewski combines cut paper and collage in *The Warrior and the Wise Man*.

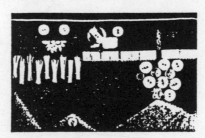

Printmaking

Shapes can be repeated through printmaking. Students can dip cut-out vegetables, wood, found objects, lace doilies, etc. in paint and then press them against paper to make repeated shapes and textures in their illustrations.

They can imitate the style of Ashley Wolff's glowing block prints in *A Year of Birds*, Blair Lent's cardboard cutouts in *Bayberry Bluff*, Maria Horvath's linoleum-cut illustrations in Maggie Duff's *Dancing Turtle*, and Leo Lionni's in *Swimmy*.

Printing with woodcuts can create interesting patterns: bold lines, dramatic textures, and rich grains appear as students cut a design into a wooden surface, roll ink on the raised portion, and then print it on paper. Tejima creates breathtaking woodcuts in his glimpses of the natural world in *Owl Lake, Swan Sky, Fox's Dream,* and *Woodpecker Forest*, Dale De Armond uses striking black, red, and white woodcuts in his Inuit legend, *Berry Woman's Children*, and Ashley Bryan's woodcuts enhance the African motif in *Lion and the Ostrich Chicks and Other African Folk Tales*.

Cut Paper

Cutting folded paper adds intricate details to papercraft constructions. Simply folding a piece of paper and cutting repeated symmetrical shapes in it creates a three-dimensional shape that can be either a character or a setting. Ed Young's unusual and vibrant illustrations in Jane Yolen's *The Emperor and the Kite* and Hou'tien Cheng's stunning scissors cuts in *Six Chinese Brothers* demonstrate an intricate oriental papercut technique.

Stitchery

Students can weave, paint, or embroider fabric to create scenes or portraits of story characters.

Cynthia and William Birrer's three-dimensional stitchery from *The Shoemaker and the Elves* can serve as a model.

Elements of Design

Borders

Borders can be not only aesthetically pleasing as they frame illustrations, but also build background by elaborating on the story theme. Some borders repeat cultural motifs that reflect the setting of the story. Others illustrate a subplot of the story.

For outstanding borders, students can look at Trina Schart Hyman's *Little Red Riding Hood*, Mercer Mayer's *Sleeping Beauty*, Nonny Hogrogian's *Cinderella*, Rumer Godden's *The Dragon of Og*, Errol le Cain's tapestry borders in *Beauty and the Beast* and ornate patterns in *Aladdin*, Laszlo Gal's lavishly decorated borders in Eva Martin's *Canadian Fairy Tales*, and Jan Piénkowski's gilt borders in *Christmas — The King James Version*. Students can also compare different interpretations of *Goldilocks and the Three Bears* — Jan Brett's intricate patterns versus Lynn Bywaters Ferris's folk designs in Armand Eisen's version of the Grimm classic.

Endpapers

Some picture books have decorated endpapers, the first and last pages in a book that are attached to the front and back covers. Some endpapers are simply designs while others repeat symbols from the story.

Examples of marbled endpapers can be seen in Nonny Hogrogian's *The Glass Mountain*, patterned wallpaper in Leo Lionni's *Let's Make Rabbits*, Marcia Sewall's silhouettes in Lore Segal's *The Story of Old Mrs. Brubeck and How She Looked for Trouble and Where She Found Him*, and splashes of paint in Eric Carle's *The Very Busy Spider* and *The Tiny Seed* and in Alice McLerran's *The Mountain That Loved a Bird*. Tony Ross illustrates rows of pigs in *The Three Little Pigs*, Jan Brett uses colorful story symbols in Eve Bunting's *Scary, Scary Halloween*, Winfried Opgenoorth decorates with stylized snowflakes in Mira Lobe's *The Snowman Who Went for a Walk*, Paul Zelinsky uses panoramic scenes in *Rumpelstiltskin*, and Sandra and Michel Laroche create a snow rose symbol for *The Snow Rose*. Older students can observe how Taro Yashima uses endpapers to symbolize the theme of the story in *Crow Boy*.

Some books incorporate a map in the endpapers, as in Ted Harrison's illustrations for Robert Service's *The Shooting of Dan McGrew*, Peter Cross's *Trouble for Trumpets*, and Chris Conover's *Mother Goose and the Sly Fox*.

How to Make a Hardcover Book

MATERIALS NEEDED:

Cardboard
Durable cover material: fabric, wallpaper, or contact paper

White glue
Heavy string or dental floss
Colorful paper to serve as endpapers

1. Cut two pieces of cardboard the same size.

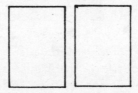

2. Place cover material face down.
   With a pencil, draw a margin along all sides.

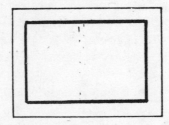

3. Glue one piece of cardboard within the edges of the *left* side of the cover.

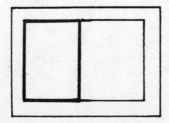

4. Glue the other piece of cardboard within the edges on the *right* side of the paper.

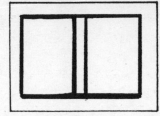

5. Fold the four corners over and glue in place.

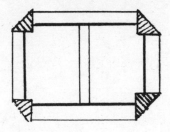

6. Then fold all four sides over and glue.

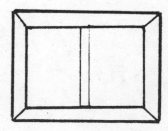

7. Cut paper to be slightly smaller than the cover. Cut two sheets of colorful paper the same size and set aside as endpapers.

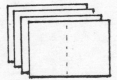 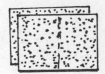

8. Fold the book pages and use heavy string or dental floss to sew them together.

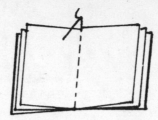

9. Glue the sewn pages into the cover. Glue the endpapers, colored face up, binding the cover and the first, then the last page of the text to them.

Paper Engineering

Some picture books have flaps to lift up and peek under, wheels to rotate, scenes that pop up, cut-out pages that overlay, fold-out panoramas, and pictures that move. Many of these three-dimensional illustrations are for clarity and interest in helping develop concepts in informational texts. They often combine a variety of paper constructions and can be used as models for students to observe before trying their own.

The process of paper engineering provides opportunities for students to use many thinking skills: observing, hypothesizing, comparing, organizing, applying, and expanding the ability to reason logically. Paper engineering engages students in applying their measurement skills, since they must be careful in constructing their designs. The process is more important than the end product.

Lift-a-Flaps

Lift-a-flaps reinforce readers' interaction with the text. Some flaps lift to conceal hidden messages or concealed clues that involve readers in some way.

Robert Crowther's *The Most Amazing Hide-and-Seek Alphabet Book* and *The Most Amazing Hide-and-Seek Counting Book* include flaps that cleverly conceal objects used for identifying respectively the letters of the alphabet and numbers. Peter Seymour and John Wallner's *The Three Little Pigs* and *Sleeping Beauty* incorporate lift-a-flap rebus stories that give students context clues for word recognition.

Flaps need to be made from sturdy paper. The size and shape depend on the story.

1. Cut a flap in any shape.

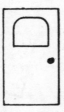

2. Fold back a strip on one side of the flap.

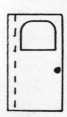

3. Paste the strip only to the background.

4. Add details by drawing something under the flap.

Fold-outs

Fold-out constructions open up to create panoramic scenes. Helen Craig's *Mouse House Months* follows a tree through the seasons, while Naomi Russell's *The Tree* traces the life cycle of an oak tree. David Peters's fold-out pages depict gargantuan animals in *Giants of Land, Sea and Air*. John Norris Wood and Kevin Dean's *Nature Hide and Seek: Jungles* and *Nature Hide and Seek: Oceans* use fold-outs that help readers locate and identify information.

Fold-out panoramic scenes can be created by using sheets of paper that are wider than the width of the final book pages.

1. A jungle scene can be created by drawing a scene on the background which covers the entire sheet of paper.

2. Fold the side edges over and continue drawing, illustrating the foreground scene.

3. The overlapping edges can be cut out to simulate the details of foliage or leaves.

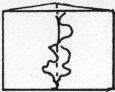

4. When the book is read, the fold-outs open to reveal a hidden scene.

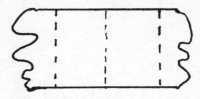

Pop-ups

Pop-ups surprise readers through animating figures or scenes which pop up when pages are opened. Jan Piénkowski's *Gossip* and *Haunted House*, the adaptation of Beatrix Potter's *Peter Rabbit*, Barbara Cooney's adaptation of Sergei Prokofiev's *Peter and the Wolf*, David Carter's *Surprise Party*, Tomie de Paola's *Georgio's Village*, or John Goodall's *Shrewbettina Goes to Work* and *Lavinia's Cottage* are good models.

Pop-up construction is also used in many content area books as it provides the depth needed to understand three-dimensional concepts. Alice and Martin Provensen use three-dimensional movable pictures for their book *Leonardo Da Vinci*, Ib Penick uses complex engineering in Seymour Reit's *Those Fabulous Flying Machines*, John Bradley's flaps, moving diagrams, and pop-ups explain the workings of an airplane in Ray Marshall's *The Plane*, Mitsumasa Anno's three-dimensional pop-ups invite readers to experiment with the sun and shadows in *Anno's Sundial*, Graham Tarrant's pop-ups present the metamorphosis of a tadpole in *Frogs*, and David Pelham's pop-ups reveal more about human anatomy than flat pictures ever could in Jonathan Miller's *The Human Body*.

Use heavier paper for pop-up construction.

1. Cut out any shape or scene that can pop up when the book is open.

2. Fold over 1 cm. along the bottom edge of the pop-up scene or shape.

3. Use another piece of paper folded in half for the background page. Illustrate the background page to match the pop-up images.

4. Paste along the folded strip of the pop-up shape and fasten it to the background scene.

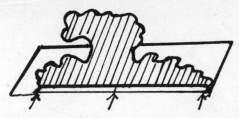

5. Open the pop-up scene.

Wheels

Wheels embedded in pages can be rotated to demonstrate a change in a scene or present an animated action. Pam Adams's *There Were Ten in the Bed* works well in helping younger students learn to count.

Pages with wheels should be made of durable paper. The wheel portion can be made of oak tag or a paper of heavy construction.

1. Use a large piece of paper and make a crease down the middle.

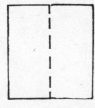

2. Cut out a wheel window on the right side of the paper.

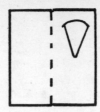

3. Cut out a wheel shape and illustrate it with scenes that are equally spaced apart. Punch out a hole in the centre (•) of the wheel.

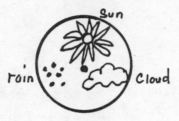

4. Secure a paper fastener through the hole in the wheel (•) and through the back cover.

5. Fold the paper along the crease and glue the two outside corners shut.

Dioramas

Dioramas create fascinating three-dimensional settings that allow older students to combine writing and art with measurement skills. Using three five-frame, accordion-pleated folds, openings are cut into the frames to create scenes that narrow rather like a peep show illusion. When a diorama book is opened, its two covers can be tied back together to create a carousel effect. Mary McClain's *Hansel and Gretel* highlights three-dimensional scenes from the popular tale in a diorama book. Variations include Molly Bang's illustrations in *The Paper Crane*, which are photographs of three dimensional paper cut-out dioramas, and Giles Laroche's paper construction, which literally adds depth to Lois Lenski's poem, *Sing a Song of People*.

A diorama usually consists of three layers of accordion folds fastened to lie on top of each other.

Materials:
3 sheets of heavy construction paper 16 cm high by (1) 90 cm., (2) 72 cm., (3) 62 cm. long
1 sturdy book cover
2 15-cm. shoestring ties

1. Background section: Fold one sheet of paper 90 cm. long into 10 accordion-pleated folds.

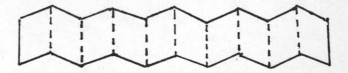

Middle section: Fold one sheet of paper 72 cm. long into 10 accordion-pleated folds (this length includes 1 cm. at each end to fold over and glue to back cover).

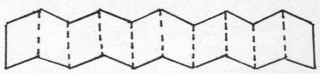

105

Foreground section: Fold one sheet of paper 62 cm. long into 10 accordion-pleated folds (this also includes 1 cm. at each end to fold over and glue to back cover).

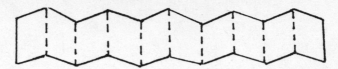

2. Select five scenes to illustrate, one for each of the accordion folds. Each scene will have three layers: a background scene, a middle scene, and a foreground scene. Progressively smaller openings are cut into the foreground and middle sections respectively to give the scene a dimensional effect. The background layer is not cut at all.

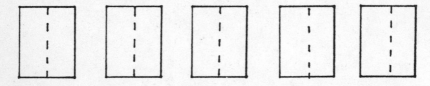

3. Draw the background of the first scene on the first back accordion fold, then draw a scene containing a middle scene character or setting on the first accordion fold of the middle section. Finally, draw a scene with a foreground character on the first fold of the foreground section. Follow the same procedure for the four remaining accordion folds. Use sharp scissors to cut openings in the middle and foreground sections, cutting out around outlines of characters or scenes. When the accordion folds are overlaid, they form the diorama.

Background scene

Middle scene

Foreground scene

4. To assemble the diorama book: glue 2 15-cm. lengths of shoe-string cord halfway down each side edge cover; fold over 1 cm. at each end of the middle accordion-folded layer and the foreground accordion folded layer; then glue the background accordion-folded layer to the side edge of the cover, then the folded ends of the middle layer to the side edge of the background, and finally the folded ends of the foreground layer to the side edge of the middle layer.

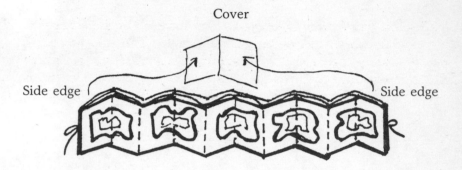

Cover

Side edge

Side edge

5. When the book is opened and tied cover to cover, it looks like a carousel.

Whether or not your students' art activities lead to making books, they will enrich experience across the curriculum. Tying language and literature to the senses will radically improve the meaning students make. Sight is only one sense. We turn now to another: hearing.

CHAPTER SIX

Music

As we have seen, reading aloud, listening, and talking all bring literature alive. A more specialized, but no less rich, kind of auditory experience that can be incorporated into your classroom is music. Musical experiences can contribute to language learning as students participate in listening, singing, clapping, moving to music, and using percussive or other instruments.

Songs

Many picture books are illustrated versions of familiar songs. Whole language teachers often combine a story sharing with the singing of a song. Favorite Mother Goose rhymes and songs like Sarah Josepha Hale's *Mary Had a Little Lamb* and Peter Spier's *London Bridge Is Falling Down* can help emerging readers "read" a text. Students practise reading-like behaviors as they match lyrics they already know with words and phrases in a book or as they are pointed to and repeated on a chart.

For Beginning Learners: Share John Langstaff's *Frog Went A-*

Courtin' and *Oh, A' Hunting We Will Go*, Pete Seeger's *Foolish Frog*, Peter Spier's *Fox Went Out on a Chilly Night*, Aliki's *Go Tell Aunt Rhody* and *Hush Little Baby*, Marcia Sewall's *Animal Song*, Robin Koontz's *This Old Man: The Counting Song*, and Robert Quakenbush's *Old MacDonald Had a Farm*. Some other stories, such as Robert Munsch's *I'll Love You Forever*, have music-like refrains that invite student participation.

For Developing Learners: Share Jan Brett's *The Twelve Days of Christmas*, Susan Jeffers's *All the Pretty Little Horses*, Peter Spier's *The Erie Canal*, Shel Silverstein's *Unicorn Song*, Marcia Sewall's *Ridin' That Strawberry Roan*, or folk songs from Scott Sanders's *Hear the Wind Blow*. An alternate suggestion is to have students write new lyrics for familiar songs that have a highly repetitive pattern.

Ballads

Ballads are narrative poems that have been adapted to folk songs about heroic deeds. They are usually characterized by strong rhythms and refrains and are often sung to a stringed accompaniment. Some popular ballads that students may recognize have appeared in book form.

For Beginning Learners: Students can sing and mime the actions in John Langstaff's picture book of the sea chanty, *The Golden Vanity*, or "The Ballad of John Henry" in Ruth Seeger's *American Folk Songs for Children*. Other song-stories are Richard Chase's *Billy Boy*, and Glen Rounds's *Casey Jones* or *The Strawberry Roan*.

For Developing Learners: Older students can set Robert Service's *The Cremation of Sam McGee* to music or summarize a book by writing a ballad about it. They might try writing a ballad about Vesper Holly from Lloyd Alexander's *The Jedera Adventure*, making up their own tune or using the melody of a familiar ballad but changing the words.

Percussive Instruments

Students can make a storytelling more dramatic by playing along to a story with percussive instruments like drums, rhythm sticks, tambourines, triangles, tone bells, or sand blocks. This adds to "sound stories" that have a strong rhythmic element.

For Beginning Learners: Rhythm instruments can be used for the "trip/trap/trip/trap" refrain in Paul Galdone's *The Three Billy Goats Gruff* or the "teeny-tiny" refrain in *The Teeny-Tiny Woman*, for the sounds and motions in Linda Williams's *The Little Old Lady Who Was Not Afraid of Anything*, Marilyn Kovalski's *Wheels on the Bus*, and Arlene Mosel's *The Funny Little Woman*, for creating sound effects in Verna Aardema's Liberian tale *The Vingananee and the Tree Toad* and *Rabbit Makes a Monkey of Lion*, Richard Fowler's *Mr. Little's Noisy 1 2 3* and Benjamin Allan's *Rat-a-Tat, Pitter Pat*, for the animal noises in Pat Hutchins's *Good Night Owl*, Wilson Gage's *Down in the Boondocks*, Wesley Porter's *The Musicians of Bremen*, Diane Stanley's *Fiddle-I-Fee*, Valerie Scho Carey's *Quail Song*, or Joanna Cole's *It's Too Noisy*. A drum can accompany Maggie Duff's *Rum Pum Pum*, and Jack Prelutsky's humorous poem "Pumberly Pott's Unpredictable Niece" from *The Queen of Eene* invites instrumental accompaniment.

For Developing Learners: Create rhythmic sound effects in Ernest Thayer's *Casey at the Bat* and Katherine Paterson's translation of *The Crane Wife*, or add a stringed sound to Dennis Hasely's *The Old Banjo*. Poetry selections by Jack Prelutsky in *The New Kid on the Block* and *Rolling Harvey Down the Hill*, or Dennis Lee's nonsense verses in *Alligator Pie* and *Garbage Delight*, have strong rhythmic beats and work well with rhythmic accompaniment.

Musical Dramatizations

Music can serve as the background to a story reading. You should select a musical composition that blends in rhythm, pace, and mood with the story to be shared. If the story does not work with the pacing of the music, you can still enhance the mood by playing the musical selection before and after reading the story.

For Beginning Learners: Share Selina Hastings's adaptation of Sergei Prokofiev's *Peter and the Wolf* with a recording of the music, Donald Crews's *Parade* with a march by John Philip Sousa or Crews's *Carousel* with a recording of carousel music. "The Young Prince and The Young Princess" movement from Rimsky-Korsakov's *Scheherazade* works very well with many folktales of enchantment. If you are reading a multicultural story, such as Sumiko Yagawa's *The Crane Wife* or Pam Newton's *The Stonecutter: An Indian Folktale*, try finding music that reflects the rhythmic patterns of that culture.

For Developing Learners: Most literature for older students may be too long to read in one sitting, so picture books or poems work better. Students enjoy Byrd Baylor's *Hawk, I'm Your Brother* accompanied by the soundtrack recording of "Born Free", or use a drum to keep the beat with her anthology of free verse, *Desert Voices*. Sharing E.T. Hoffmann's *Nutcracker* would not be complete without playing a recording of the music.

Music can also nurture story writing. Try having students listen to a recording of jazz, pop, or classical music — symphonic, operatic, etc. — and then record the visual images it inspires in them. After drawing a series of pictures that are triggered by the music, the students can write a story to accompany the pictures.

Another way to combine most music and story is to create a "sound scape". During a story reading, students can use musical instruments to create complementary sound effects that mesh in a sort of musical composition.

For instance, while reading a story in which there is a rainstorm, students can score a sound scape that simulates the sounds by plucking, striking, or hitting rhythm instruments.

Light rain   Heavy rain

Wind   Thunder and lightning

All these sounds can be orchestrated, one group of students performing the rain and storm while another group of students mimes storm actions.

This exercise leads naturally into the area of dramatization, the final and perhaps most comprehensive extension of literature in the classroom.

CHAPTER SEVEN

Storytelling and Drama

Drama in the classroom can incorporate virtually every activity described in previous chapters: reading, writing, art, music, and more. It can range from spontaneous improvisation to formal presentation of a scripted play, and can include a range of costumes, props, and sets, musical accompaniment, mime, or dance — or none of the above. Informal drama emphasizes the improvising or composing process, while formal drama emphasizes a relatively polished production.

Storytelling is a valuable activity in itself, but can also be used as a way to develop students' awareness of the dramatic possibilities of stories. It is a good place to start here.

Storytelling

Storytelling provides students with an opportunity to organize their thoughts, communicate effectively with others, and get actively involved in literature — their own or others'. It also helps them become familiar with story language and structures in a meaningful context. Practice in retelling encourages students to become more articulate as speakers, to make meaning as readers, and to think about composing stories themselves. Whole language teachers use storytelling activities for both *rehearsing* and *extending* narratives.

Rehearsal

Students can tell stories as a way of concrete rehearsing of ideas that will be written down. After reading or listening to stories, many students are then expected to leap into writing their own without any time to orally rehearse. This can be daunting to some of them, including ESL students, who may be more comfortable exploring ideas orally before writing them down.

Extension

One way of examining what a student has comprehended in a story is to ask the student to retell the story that he or she has read or heard. Merely asking questions after a story draws students' attention to small portions of what they have read or heard, fragmenting the story rather than revealing it as a whole. In storytelling, students must view the entire story, consider the interrelationships of characters and events, and interpret characters' motives and actions.

Storytelling is filled with creative possibilities that can lead to drama — role-playing, dialoguing, and interpreting and weaving language developed within a social context.

Group Storytelling
Add-on Cumulative Stories

Students may feel less pressure if they start telling stories in groups rather than by themselves. Add-on cumulative stories are cooperative retellings in which students take turns composing sequential parts of a story which has been initiated by the teacher, the opening of an existing story, or one of the students. Students must listen to the previous sequence and respond appropriately. For a story like Beatrix Potter's *The Tale of Peter Rabbit*, the teacher might begin:

114

Once upon a time there were four little rabbits,
and their names were . . .

Each student, perhaps sitting in a circle, would then continue the story by adding a sentence about the next event until the story is complete.

At first, students will likely follow a story they know closely, but as they gain familiarity with the activity, they may introduce "twists" to the story, which can lead to entirely original creations.

Text: They lived with their mother in a sand-bank,
      underneath the root of a very big fir tree.

Storyteller: They lived with their mother on the
             twenty-third floor of a Toronto highrise!

In composing new narratives, story devices such as a story chain (a ball of wool marked intermittently with bows to indicate story twists and turns) or objects such as a button, a sea-shell, or a key are good ways to spark students' imaginations.

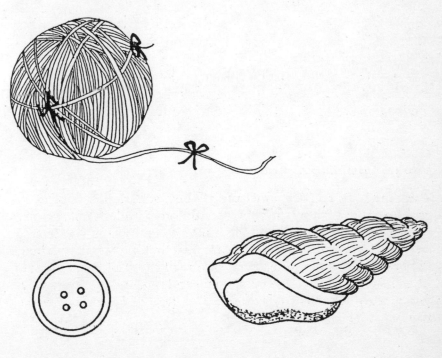

Individual Storytelling
Picture Reading

Picture reading is the easiest way to start students storytelling individually. As we have seen, whole language teachers can use pictures from storybooks or wordless books as stimuli for original stories. Wordless books and picture stories can encourage students to interpret visual material, sequence and express their ideas, and compose new stories.

For Beginning Storytellers: Younger storytellers can tell a story as they turn the pages of any number of attractive picture books — or whatever interests them.

Students can also use wordless picture books that follow a simple story sequence, such as Brinton Turkel's *Deep in the Forest*, Peter Spier's *Dreams*, or Ed Young's *The Other Bone*, to narrate an interpretation.

For Developing Storytellers: Older students can use wordless (or almost wordless) books such as Erich Fuch's *Journey to the Moon*, Chris Van Allsburg's *The Mysteries of Harris Burdick*, or Lynd Ward's *The Silver Pony* to narrate a story.

An alternate idea would be to have students create their own wordless books for high adventure short stories or for exciting chapters from longer novels. Students can orally narrate the stories shown in the picture sequences. Some students may want to tape their stories and place the tapes in the listening centre with their wordless books.

Storytelling with Props

Once they feel comfortable telling stories, students can begin to use props to make stories come alive. The props can be stored in a "Storytelling Centre" where students can find them. A few common and useful props are sequence clotheslines, flannelboards, story aprons, story boxes, story chains, masks, puppets, sequence boards, and miscellaneous objects to trigger ideas.

Story Quilt

A "Story Quilt" usually consists of a felt background scene and

116

puppets that can be used with either group or individual story-telling to help beginning storytellers map their story sequences. Using small felt puppets, they can orally describe their stories while moving the puppets around on the background scene. Puppets provide students with concrete characters with which to rehearse their ideas.

Commercial story quilts are available, but you can make your own and encourage students to make puppets themselves.

Storytelling Chair

One chair can be designated as a "storyteller's chair", a place for sharing stories. Students can tell stories they have read, stories they have written, or stories they have in progress.

Storytelling Game: Story Maker

"Story Maker" is a card game you can make that encourages students to produce "branching stories" that have alternative settings, characters, dialogue, events, and endings. The game contains cards which are arranged into four groups: setting, characters, dialogue, and events. The student task is to draw a card from each group and use them to create a scene in an add-on story sequence.

A narrator starts the add-on story by composing a story beginning:

"As I was walking on a dark path. . ."

Then each player in turn draws four cards and adds a scene to the story.

Setting	Character	Dialogue	Event
On a dark path	Monster	"What's for dinner?"	A bicycle race

Informal Drama

Informal drama includes activities in which students improvise, role-play, mime, and dramatize stories. It is really just a step beyond storytelling.

Dramatizing Stories

Students can choose familiar stories to act out, using both dialogue and body movements. There need not be a script — actors may improvise their lines — but the plot should follow the original.

A well written story with some kind of conflict and a fair

amount of action provides good material for dramatization. Good dialogue can also be important as some students are not adept at improvising dialogue.

For Beginning Readers: Folktales are excellent for dramatizations as they are short and usually feature lots of action, quick plots, and interesting characters. Share Paul Galdone's *The Three Wishes, What's in Fox's Sack?*, and *The Little Red Hen*, Anita Lobel's *The Straw Maid*, Jill Bennett's *Teeny Tiny*, Margot Zemach's *It Could Always Be Worse*, and Arnold Lobel's *Ming Lo Moves the Mountain*. Somewhat longer picture books such as Walter de la Mare's *Molly Whuppie*, Anthea Bell's *The Brave Little Tailor*, Verna Aardema's *Princess Gorilla and a New Kind of Water: A Mpongwe Tale*, and Harve Zemach's *Duffy and the Devil* also make excellent material to dramatize.

For Developing Readers: Older students can dramatize a scene or a single chapter from junior fiction. Beverly Cleary's *Ramona the Pest* and *Henry Huggins*, Betsy Byars's *The Night Swimmers*, and Elaine Konigsburg's *From the Mixed-Up Files of Mrs. Basil E. Frankweiler* are all good for dramatizing. Whatever book you use, you may want to guide students by asking them to dramatize a scene in which a major story character has to make a decision, the most humorous scene in the story, or the climax.

Improvisation

Improvisations are brief scenarios acted out with minimal planning and spontaneous dialogue. They can result in entirely new stories, but may also involve characters or situations drawn from literature. When improvisations are completed, students may talk about what happened and how they felt. They often repeat improvisations, exploring different actions and resolutions.

Teachers can help students to focus on the important problems or conflicts which characters face in literature by providing opportunities to explore these ideas. Such exploration helps students discover how different factors influence story characters.

For Beginning Readers: Share Barbara Berger's *Grandfather Twilight*, Holly Kellery's *Geraldine's Blanket*, Janina Domanska's *What Happens Next?*, or Charlotte Pomerantz's *Whiff, Sniff, Nibble and Chew: The Gingerbread Boy Retold*, and ask students to create new situations or problems for the story characters to solve.

For Developing Readers: Older students can create and dramatize a sequel or a new event in a story. Share Jan Slepian's *The Broccoli Tapes*, Jean Little's *Mama's Going to Buy You a Mockingbird*, or Eleanor Clymer's *The Get-Away Car*, and ask students to create a new event in each.

An alternate suggestion would be to have students take an interesting event from a story and dramatize it in another time period. Dramatize an incident about Sara in Esther Hautzig's *A Gift for Mama*, placing her in modern times, or an adventure for Christopher Columbus from Jan Fritz's *Where Do You Think You're Going Christopher Columbus?* on a future space exploration.

Mime

In mime, students use only their bodies and movements to convey meaning.

Whether it is their story or another, students can mime the actions of a story while a narrator reads. Later, they can mime the story interpreting it totally through action (without a narrator) and then mime a new ending or a sequel to it.

For Beginning Readers: Stories that lend themselves to beginning mime activities include Nonny Hogrogian's *One Fine Day*, Pat Hutchins's *Happy Birthday Sam* and *The Doorbell Rang*, Marcia Brown's *Stone Soup*, Ezra Jack Keats's *The Snowy Day*, John Burningham's *Time to Get Out of the Bath, Shirley*, Mirra Ginsburg's *Mushroom in the Rain* and *How the Sun Was Brought Back to the Sky*, and Elizabeth Shrub's translation of the Grimm Brothers' *The Bremen Town Musicians*.

For Developing Readers: Picture storybooks work better for mime activities, as their plots are shorter than those in junior fiction. Students can use mime to show how story events change characters. Tomie de Paola's *Fin M'Coul: The Giant of Knockmany Hill* and Gerald McDermott's *The Stonecutter* have exciting story actions and memorable characters to mime. Students can show how one character walks, another feels, and another looks.

An alternate suggestion would be to have students mime scenes from a tape-recorded story or scene. Ask older students to mime

Jess and Leslie walking through the two settings in *Bridge to Terabithia*: the world of home and school, and the secret world of Terabithia.

Role-playing

In role-playing, a student takes on the role of a character and then reacts to a situation as he or she thinks the character would. Role-playing involves the ability to understand the viewpoint of another person.

Realistic fiction allows students to empathize with story characters who have problems that many students might experience. Through role-playing, they may discover ways to handle problems and increase their sensitivity to the problems of others while at the same time developing their own personal value systems.

For Beginning Readers: Students can role-play Simon's problem in Betty Waterton's *Salmon for Simon*, Sara's in Esther Hautzig's *A Gift for Mama*, or Peter's in Ann McGovern's *Too Much Noise*.

For Developing Readers: Older students can role-play an episode from Jean Merrill's *The Pushcart War* as pushcart peddlers unite in their struggles, or the episode from Jean Craighead George's *My Side of the Mountain* when a news reporter comes to interview Sam. They can conduct a television interview with their favorite story characters, asking Dicey Tillerman from *Dicey's Song* about the problems she had adjusting to living with her grandmother, talking to James Johnson about the fears he had when he moved away from his grandmother and became known as Jimmy Jo in Katherine Paterson's *Come Sing, Jimmy Jo*, or asking Meg Murray to describe what she saw as she was whisked through time and space aboard the back of Mrs. Whatsit in Madeleine L'Engle's *A Wrinkle in Time*.

Formal Drama

Formal drama requires a script, and possibly costumes, props, sets, and music. Although students must try to memorize and rehearse, you should emphasize the enjoyment of language and literature rather than the perfect memorizing of lines.

Depending on how elaborate your production is, it may take days or weeks to prepare: it is a good idea to start with simple, very short dramas and gradually build up to more complex ones.

Story Theatre

Story theatre is the performance of a script, based on a literary selection, that has been rehearsed. It emphasizes the oral interpretation of literature, and helps students develop an understanding of story characters as they interpret the characters through dialogue and actions. The best stories for story theatre are those with vividly portrayed characters and lots of dialogue.

For Beginning Readers: Repetitive stories are useful in this activity, as their story lines are the easiest to remember. Verna Aardema's *Who's in Rabbit's House* is written like a dramatic script; Paul Galdone's *The Little Red Hen* and George Shannon's *Piney Woods Peddler* follow a predictable sequence; and stories like Tomie dePaola's *Strega Nona* and Paul Galdone's *The Magic Porridge Pot* include lines that are easy to remember.

For Developing Readers: Older students can write their own scripts based on stories they have read. Shorter books are a good beginning. Diane Wolkstein's *The Magic Wings: A Tale from China* offers suggestions for writing a story script, and these can be used as a model for other scripts. As students develop as readers, they can script a short episode from a longer adventure story such as James Houston's *Frozen Fire* or *Black Diamonds*, or a fantasy story set in another world, such as Lloyd Alexander's *Taran Wanderer*.

Conclusion

The activities and literature I have described in this book are just a starting point. With time and experience, you and your students will discover other wonderful picture books, stories, poems, scripts, and non-fiction, and will invent enriching experiences to go with them. And the more varied the literature and activities, the more complex and extensive the web that ties children not only to literature but to each other and the world around them.

Bibliography

Chapter 1: Listening and Talking

Baylor, Byrd. *The Best Town in the World*. Ronald Himler, illustrator. New York: Charles Scribner's Sons, 1983.

Bonne, Rose. *I Know an Old Lady*. New York: Scholastic, 1985.

Dee, Ruby. *Two Ways to Count to Ten: A Liberian Folktale*. Susan Meddugh, illustrator. New York: Henry Holt, 1988.

Deming, A.G. *Who Is Tapping at My Window?* Marcia Wellington, illustrator. New York: E.P. Dutton, 1988.

Domanska, Janina. *Busy Monday Morning*. New York: Greenwillow, 1985.

Fox, Paula. *Lily and the Lost Boy*. New York: Orchard, 1987.

Galdone, Joanna. *The Tailypo*. Paul Galdone, illustrator. New York: Clarion, 1977.

Ginsburg, Mirra. *The Magic Stove*. Linda Heller, illustrator. New York: Coward McCann, 1983.

Hall, Amanda. *The Gossipy Wife*. New York: P. Bedrick, 1984.

Halvorson, Marilyn. *Cowboys Don't Cry*. Toronto: Irwin, 1984.

Hazen, Barbara Shook. *Tight Times*. New York: Penguin, 1983.

Hutchins, Pat. *Don't Forget the Bacon*. New York: Penguin, 1978.

Johnson, Jane. *Today I Thought I'd Run Away*. London: A.C. Black, 1985.

Kellogg, Steven. *The Island of the Skog*. New York: Dial, 1976.

Laurence, Margaret. *The Olden Days Coat*. Margaret Wood, illustrator. Toronto: McClelland and Stewart, 1979.

Major, Kevin. *Blood Red Ochre*. Toronto: Doubleday, 1989.

Mayer, Mercer. *What Do You Do with a Kangaroo?* New York: Scholastic, 1973.

Marshall, Edward. *Space Case*. James Marshall, illustrator. New York: Dial, 1980.

Mowat, Farley. *Owls in the Family*. Robert Frankenberg, illustrator. Toronto: McClelland and Stewart, 1973.

Munsch, Robert. *Jonathan Cleaned Up — Then He Heard a Sound, or Blackberry Subway Jam*. Michael Martchenko, illustrator. Toronto: Annick, 1981.

Nerlove, Miriam. *I Made a Mistake*. New York: Atheneum, 1985.

O'Connor, Jane. *The Teeny Tiny Woman*. R.W. Alley, illustrator. New York: Random House, 1986.

Provensen, Alice and Martin. *The Glorious Flight across the Channel with Louis Blériot, July 25, 1909*. New York: Viking, 1983.

Radin, Ruth Yaffe. *A Winter Place*. Mattie Lou O'Kelly, illustrator. New York: Little, Brown, 1982.

Ross, Tony. *Lazy Jack*. New York: Dial, 1986.

San Souci, Robert. *The Enchanted Tapestry*. Lazlo Gal, illustrator. New York: Dial, 1987.

Siebert, Diannne. *Mojave*. Wendell Minor, illustrator. New York: Thomas Y. Crowell, 1988.

Simmie, Lois. *An Armadillow Is Not a Pillow*. Anne Simmie, illustrator. Saskatoon: Western Producer Prairie Books, 1986.

_____. *Auntie's Knitting a Baby*. Anne Simmie, illustrator. Saskatoon: Western Producer Prairie Books, 1986.

Simon, Seymour. *Jupiter*. New York: William Morrow, 1985.

_____. *Saturn*. New York: William Morrow, 1985.

Slote, Alfred. *The Trouble on Janus*. James Watt, illustrator. Philadelphia: Lippincott, 1985.

Thayer, Ernest Lawrence (with additional text by Patricia Polacco). *Casey at the Bat: A Ballad of the Republic, Sung in the Year 1888*. Patricia Polacco, illustrator. New York: G.P. Putnam's Sons, 1982.

Turkel, Brinton. *Do Not Open*. New York: Elsevier/Dutton, 1983.

Uchida, Yoshiko. *The Two Foolish Cats*. Margot Zemach, illustrator. New York: Atheneum, 1987.

Waber, Bernard. *"You Look Ridiculous" Said the Hippopotamus to the Rhinoceros*. New York: Houghton Mifflin, 1966.

Wadsworth, Olive A. *Over in the Meadow: A Counting-Out Rhyme*. Mary Maki Rae, illustrator. New York: Viking, 1985.

Weiss, Nicki. *Dog Boy Cap Skate*. New York: Greenwillow, 1989.

_____. *An Egg Is an Egg*. New York: G.P. Putnam's Sons, 1990.

Chapter 2: Viewing

Adams, Pam, and Ceri Jones. *I Thought I Saw*. London: Child's Play, 1974.

Adkins, Jan. *Inside: Seeing beneath the Surface*. New York: Walker & Co., 1975.

Ahlberg, Allen and Janet. *Each Peach Pear Plum: An I Spy Story*. New York: Viking, 1978.

Aliki. *A Medieval Feast*. New York: Thomas Y. Crowell, 1983.

Allen, Pamela. *Who Sank the Boat?* New York: Coward, McCann, & Geoghegan, 1983.

Anno, Mitsumasa. *Anno's Britain*. New York: Philomel, 1982.

_____. *Anno's Italy*. New York: Collins, 1980.

_____. *Anno's Journey*. New York: Philomel, 1978.

_____. *Topsy-Turvies*. New York: Philomel, 1989.

Aruego, José, and Ariane Dewey. *We Hide, You Seek*. New York: Greenwillow, 1979.

Bailey, Jill. *Animals of Course! Eyes.* Oxford Scientific Films, photographs. New York: G.P. Putnam's Sons, 1984.

Brown, Ruth. *If At First You Do Not See*. New York: Holt, Rinehart and Winston, 1982.

Catalanatto, Peter. *Dylon's Day Out*. New York: Franklin Watts, 1989.

Chwast, Seymour. *Tall City, Wide Country*. New York: Viking, 1983.

Cole, Joanna. *Cars and How They Go*. Gail Gibbons, illustrator. New York: Harper and Row, 1983.

Cross, Peter. *Trouble for Trumpets*. New York: Random House, 1984.

Gardner, Beau. *The Look Again. . . .and Again, and Again and Again Book*. New York: Lothrop, Lee and Shephard, 1983.

George, Jean. *One Day in the Woods*. Gary Allen, illustrator. New York: Thomas Y. Crowell, 1988.

Goodall, John. *The Story of an English Village*. New York: Atheneum, 1979.

Goor, Ron and Nancy. *In the Driver's Seat*. New York: Thomas Y. Crowell, 1982.

Hirschl, Ron. *Who Lives on . . . the Prairie?* Galen Barrell, illustrator. New York: G.P. Putnam's Sons, 1989.

Hoban, Tina. *Is It Rough? Is It Smooth? Is It Shiny?* New York: Greenwillow, 1984.

_____. *Round and Round and Round*. New York: Greenwillow, 1983.

_____. *Take Another Look*. New York: Greenwillow, 1981.

Hutchins, Pat. *One Hunter*. New York: Greenwillow, 1982.

Jonas, Ann. *Round Trip*. New York: Greenwillow, 1983.

_____. *The Trek*. New York: Greenwillow, 1985.

Littledale, Freya. *The Magic Plum Tree*. Enrico Arno, illustrator. New York: Crown, 1981.

MacDonald, Suse, and Bill Oakes. *Puzzles*. New York: 1989.

Parnall, Peter. *Winter Barn*. New York: Macmillan, 1986.

Rahn, John Elma. *Holes*. New York: Houghton Mifflin, 1984.

Ryder, Joanne. *Step into the Night*. Dennis Nolan, illustrator. New York: Four Winds Press, 1988.

Simon, Seymour. *Jupiter*. New York: William Morrow and Co., 1985.

_____. *The Long View into Space*. New York: Thomas Y. Crowell, 1979.

Simpson, Mary Jett. *Adventuring with Books*. Urbana, Ill.: The National Council of Teachers of English, 1989.

Titherington, Jeanne. *Where Are You Going Emma?* New York: Greenwillow, 1989.

Ziebel, Peter. *Look Closer!* New York: Clarion, 1989.

Zisfein, Melvin B. *Flight: A Panorama of Aviation*. Robert Andrew Parker, photographs. New York: Pantheon, 1981.

Barchas, Sarah. *I Was Walking down the Road*. New York: Scholastic, 1988.

Baylor, Byrd. *Hawk, I'm Your Brother*. Peter Parnall, illustrator. New York: Scribner's Sons, 1975.

_____. *The Other Way to Listen*. Peter Parnall, illustrator. New York: Scribner's Sons, 1978.

Bennett, Jill. *Noisy Poems*. Nick Sharratt, illustrator. New York: Oxford, 1989.

Blos, Joan. *Lottie's Circus*. Irene Trevor, illustrator. New York: Morrow, 1989.

Bourgeois, Paulette. *Franklin in the Dark*. Ann Clark, illustrator. Toronto: Kids Can Press, 1986.

Brett, Jan. *The Mitten*. New York: E. P. Putnam's Sons, 1989.

Brown, Ruth. *The Big Sneeze*. New York: Lothrop, Lee and Shepard, 1985.

Byars, Betsy. *Midnight Fox*. Negri Rocco, illustrator. New York: Penguin, 1989.

_____. *Trouble River*. New York: Scholastic, 1967.

Calhoun, Mary. *Julie's Tree*. New York: Harper and Row, 1988.

Clark, Ann Nolan. *In the Land of the Small Dragon*. Tony Chen, illustrator. New York: Viking, 1979.

Climo, Shirley. *The Egyptian Cinderella*. Ruth Heller, illustrator. New York: Thomas Y. Crowell, 1989.

Cole, Joanna. *It's Too Noisy*. Kate Duke, illustrator. New York: Thomas Y. Crowell, 1989.

Crowe, Robert. *Clyde Monster*. Kay Charo, illustrator. New York: E.P. Dutton, 1976.

Eyvindson, Peter. *Circus Berserkus*. Doug J. Keith, illustrator. Winnipeg: Pemmican Publications, 1989.

Fernandes, Eugenie. *A Difficult Day*. Toronto: Kids Can Press, 1987.

Fitzhugh, Louise. *Nobody's Family Is Going to Change*. New York: Dell, 1975.

Fleischman, Paul. *Joyful Noise: Poems for Two Voices*. Eric Beddows, illustrator. New York: Harper and Row, 1988.

Fleischman, Sid. *The Whipping Boy*. Peter Sis, illustrator. New York: Troll Associates/Troll Books, 1987.

Frost, Robert. *Stopping by Woods on a Snowy Evening*. Susan Jeffers, illustrator. New York: E.P. Dutton, 1978.

Gardiner, John. *Stone Fox*. Marcia Sewall, illustrator. New York: Harper and Row, 1980.

George, Jean Craighead. *Julie of the Wolves*. John Schoenherr, illustrator. New York: Harper and Row, 1972.

Gripe, Maria. *Elvis and His Secret*. Harold Gripe, illustrator. New York: Delacorte, 1976.

Haviland, Virginia, editor. "The Indian Cinderella" in *North American Legends*. Ann Strugnell, illustrator. New York: Collins, 1979.

Hogrogian, Nonny. *The Cat Who Loved to Sing*. New York: Knopf, 1988.

Holman, Felice. *Slake's Limbo*. New York: Charles S. Scribner's Sons, 1972.

Hooks, William H. *Moss Gown*. Donald Carrick, illustrator. New York: Clarion Books, 1987.

Huck, Charlotte, reteller. *Princess Furball*. Anita Lobel, illustrator. New York: E. P. Dutton, 1989.

Ishii, Momoko. (Katherine Paterson, translator.) *The Tongue-Tied Sparrow*. Suekichi Akaba, illustrator. New York: E. P. Dutton, 1987.

Jacobs, Joseph. *Tattercoats*. Margot Toms, illustrator. New York: E. P. Putnam's Sons, 1989.

Keller, Charles. *Tongue Twisters*. Ron Fritz, illustrator. New York: Simon and Schuster, 1989.

Konigsburg, Elaine. *From the Mixed-up Files of Mrs. Basil E. Frankweiler*. New York: Atheneum, 1967.

Kushner, Donn. *The Violin Maker's Gift*. Doug Panton, illustrator. New York: Farrar, Straus and Giroux, 1982.

Laskey, Kathryn. *Sugaring Time*. Christopher Knight, photographer. New York: Macmillan, 1983.

Lear, Edward. *The Owl and the Pussycat*. Janet Stevens, illustrator. New York: Holiday House, 1983.

Lobel, Arnold. *The Book of Pigericks: Pig Limericks*. New York: Harper and Row, 1983.

_____. *The Rose in My Garden*. Anita Lobel, illustrator. New York: Greenwillow, 1984.

Longfellow, Henry Wadsworth. *Hiawatha*. Susan Jeffers, illustrator. New York: Dial, 1983.

Louie, Ai-Ling. *Yeh Shen: A Cinderella Story from China*. Ed Young, illustrator. New York: Philomel, 1982.

Lowry, Lois. *All about Sam*. Diane deGroat, illustrator. New York: Houghton Mifflin, 1988.

———. *Rabble Starkey*. New York: Houghton Mifflin, 1987.

Manes, Stephen. *Be a Perfect Person in Just Three Days*. Toronto: Bantam, 1982.

Martin, Bill Jr., and John Archambault. *Barn Dance!* Ted Rand, illustrator. New York: Henry Holt, 1986.

———. *Listen to the Rain*. James Endicott, illustrator. New York: Henry Holt, 1988.

Mayer, Mercer. *There's a Nightmare in My Closet*. New York: Dial, 1968.

———. *There's an Alligator under My Bed*. New York: Dial, 1987.

McGovern, Ann. *Too Much Noise*. New York: Houghton Mifflin, 1967.

Morgan, Allan. *Nicole's Boat: A Goodnight Story*. Jirinia Marton, illustrator. Toronto: Kids Can Press, 1986.

Obed, Ellen Bryan. *Wind in My Pocket*. Shawn Steffler, illustrator. St. John's: Breakwater Books, 1990.

Oppenheim, Joanne. *You Can't Catch Me!* Andrew Schacat, illustrator. New York: Houghton Mifflin, 1986.

Oram, Hiawyn. *In the Attic*. Satoshi Kitamura, illustrator. New York: Holt, Rinehart and Winston, 1985.

———. *Ned and the Jaybaloo*. Satoshi Kitamura, illustrator. New York: Beaver Arrow Books, 1987.

Paterson, Katherine. *Come Sing, Jimmy Jo*. New York: E. P. Dutton, 1985.

Peek, Merle. *Mary Wore Her Red Dress and Henry Wore His Green Sneakers*. New York: Clarion Books, 1985.

Riley, James Whitcomb. *Little Orphant Annie*. Diane Stanley, illustrator. New York: G. P. Putnam's Sons, 1983.

Robertson, Keith. *In Search of a Sandhill Crane*. Richard Cuffari, illustrator. New York: Viking, 1973.

Rockwell, Anne. *Thump, Thump, Thump!* New York: E. P. Dutton, 1981.

San Souci, Robert D. *The Talking Eggs*. Jerry Pinkney, illustrator. New York: Dial, 1989.

Sendak, Maurice. *Where the Wild Things Are*. New York: Harper and Row, 1963.

Steptoe, John. *Mufaro's Daughters: An African Tale*. New York: Lothrop, Lee and Shepard, 1987.

Stevens, Janet. *The House That Jack Built*. New York: Holiday House, 1985.

Truss, Jan. *Jasmin*. Vancouver: Douglas and McIntyre, 1982.

Van Allsburg, Chris. *The Polar Express*. New York: Houghton Mifflin, 1985.

Voight, Cynthia. *A Solitary Blue*. New York: Atheneum, 1983.

Vuong, Lynette Dyer. *The Brocaded Slipper and Other Vietnamese Tales*. Vo-Dinh Mai, illustrator. New York: Addison Wesley, 1982.

Wahl, Jan. *Humphrey's Bear*. William Joyce, illustrator. New York: Henry Holt, 1987.

Walter, Mildred Pitts. *Brother to the Wind*. Leo and Diane Dillon, illustrators. New York: Lothrop, Lee & Shepard, 1985.

West, Colin. *The King of Kennelwick Castle*. Anne Dalton, illustrator. Philadelphia: Lippincott, 1986.

Wilder, Laura Ingalls. *Little House in the Big Woods*. Garth Williams, illustrator. New York: Harper and Row, 1953.

Wildsmith, Brian. *Goat's Trail*. New York: Knopf, 1986.

Williams, Jay. *Everybody Knows What a Dragon Looks Like*. Mercer Mayer, illustrator. New York: Four Winds Press, 1976.

Winthrop, Elizabeth. *Sledding*. Sarah Wilson, illustrator. New York: Harper and Row, 1989.

Wood, Audrey. *King Bidgood's in the Bathtub*. Don Wood, illustrator. San Diego: Harcourt Brace Jovanovich, 1985.

_____. *The Napping House*. Don Wood, illustrator. New York: Harcourt, 1984.

Wyndham, Robert. *Chinese Mother Goose Rhymes*. Ed Young, illustrator. New York: Philomel, 1982.

Yorinks, Arthur. *Hey, Al*. Richard Egielski, illustrator. New York: Farrar, Straus and Giroux, 1986.

Zemach, Margot. *It Could Always Be Worse*. New York: Scholastic, 1979.

Spider Books

Appiah, Peggy, reteller. *Tales of an Ashanti Father*. Nora Dickson, illustrator. New York: André Deutsch, 1981.

Arkhurst, Joyce Cooper. *The Adventures of Spider: West African Folk Tales*. Jerry Pinkney, illustrator. New York: Scholastic, 1987.

Climo, Shirley. *The Cobweb Christmas*. Joe Lasker, illustrator. New York: Thomas Y. Crowell, 1982.

_____. *Someone Saw a Spider: Spider Facts and Folktales*. Dirk Zimmer, illustrator. New York: Thomas Y. Crowell, 1985.

Crosby, Alex L. *Tarantulas: The Biggest Spiders*. New York: Walker and Co., 1981.

Freschet, Bernice. *The Web in the Grass*. Roger Duvoisin, illustrator. New York: Charles S. Scribner's Sons, 1972.

Heidbreder, Robert. *Don't Eat Spiders*. Karen Patkau, illustrator. Toronto: Oxford, 1985.

Joosse, Barbara. *Spiders in the Fruit Cellar*. Kay Chorao, illustrator. New York: Knopf, 1983.

Jukes, Mavis. *Like Jake and Me*. Lloyd Bloom, illustrator. New York: Knopf, 1984.

Lane, Margaret. *The Spider*. Barbara Firth, illustrator. New York: Dial, 1983.

McNulty, Faith. *The Lady and the Spider*. Bob Marshall, illustrator. New York: Harper and Row, 1986.

Paten, Dorothy Hinshaw. *Spider Magic*. New York: Holiday House, 1982.

Ryder, Joanne. *The Spider's Dance*. Robert J. Blake, illustrator. New York: Harper and Row, 1981.

Schnieper, Claudia. *Amazing Spiders*. Max Maier, illustrator. Minneapolis: Carolrhoda Books, 1989.

Selsam, Millicent E., and Joyce Hunt. *A First Look at Spiders*. Harriet Springer, illustrator. New York: Walker, 1983.

Wagner, Jenny. *Aranea: A Story about a Spider*. Ron Brooks, illustrator. New York: Bradbury Press, 1985.

Walther, Tom. *A Spider Might*. New York: Sierra Club/Scribner, 1978.

White, E.B. *Charlotte's Web*. Garth Williams, illustrator. New York: Harper and Row, 1952.

Chapter 4: Writing

Adler, C.S. *Footsteps on the Stairs*. New York: Delacorte, 1982.

Adoff, Arnold. *Birds*. Troy Howell, illustrator. New York: Harper and Row, 1982.

_____. *The Cabbages Are Chasing the Rabbits*. Janet Stevens, illustrator. San Diego: Harcourt Brace Jovanovich, 1985.

_____. *Sports Pages*. Steve Kuzma, illustrator. Philadelphia: Lippincott, 1986.

Ahenakew, Beth, and Sam Hardlotte, compilers. *Cree Legends: Story of Wesakechak*. Dennis Morrison, illustrator. Saskatoon: Saskatchewan Indian Cultural College, 1977.

Ahlberg, Janet and Allen. *The Jolly Postman*. New York: Little, Brown, 1986.

Alderson, Sue Ann. *Ida and the Wool Smugglers*. Ann Blades, illustrator. New York: Atheneum, 1988.

Alexander, Lloyd. *The Book of Three*. New York: Holt, Rinehart & Winston, 1964.

_____. *The Illyrian Adventure*. New York: E. P. Dutton, 1986.

Allard, Harry. *It's So Nice to Have a Wolf around the House*. James Marshall, illustrator. New York: Doubleday, 1977.

Anderson, Margaret. *The Journey of the Shadow Bairns*. New York: Scholastic, 1983.

Andrews, Jan. *Very Last First Time*. Ian Wallace, illustrator. Toronto: Groundwood, 1986.

Anno, Mitsumasa. *Anno's Medieval World*. New York: Philomel, 1990.

Arhurst, Joyce Cooper. *The Adventures of Spider: West African Folktales*. Jerry Pinkney, illustrator. New York: Little, Brown, 1964.

Avi. *Who Stole the Wizard of Oz?* Derek James, illustrator. New York: Knopf, 1981.

Aylesworth, Jim. *Shenandoah Noah*. Glen Rounds, illustrator. New York: Holt Rinehart and Winston, 1985.

Bang, Molly, adapter. *Tye May and the Magic Brush*. New York: Greenwillow, 1981.

Bauer, Marion Dane. *On My Honor*. New York: Clarion, 1986.

Baylor, Byrd. *Desert Voices*. Peter Parnall, illustrator. New York: Charles Scribner's Sons, 1981.

_____. *Moonsong*. Ronald Hunter, illustrator. New York: Charles Scribner's Sons, 1982.

Bedore, Bernie. *Tall Tales of Joe Mufferaw*. Toronto: Consolidated Amethyst, 1979.

Bellingham, Brenda. *Storm Child*. Toronto: Lorimer, 1985.

Bernstein, Margery, and Janet Korbin. *How the Sun Made a*

Promise and Kept It. Ed Heffernan, illustrator. New York: Charles Scribner's Sons, 1974.

Berrill, Margaret. *Chanticleer*. Jane Bottomly, illustrator. Milwaukee: Raintree, 1986.

Bierhorst, John. *Doctor Coyote: A Native American Aesop's Fables*. Wendy Watson, illustrator. New York: Macmillan, 1987.

Bjork, Christina. *Linnea in Monet's Garden*. Lena Anderson, illustrator. Toronto: R&S Books, 1987.

Blades, Ann. *Mary of Mile 18*. Montreal: Tundra, 1971.

Blos, Joan. *A Gathering of Days — A New England Girl's Journal 1830-1832*. New York: Charles Scribner's Sons, 1979.

Borcher, Elizabeth (translated and adapted by Elizabeth Shrub). *Dear Sarah*. Wilhelm Schlote, illustrator. New York: Greenwillow, 1981.

Bourgeois, Paulette. *Franklin in the Dark*. Brenda Clark, illustrator. Toronto: Kids Can Press, 1986.

Brenner, Barbara. *Wagon Wheels*. Don Bolognese, illustrator. New York: Harper and Row, 1978.

Brink, Carol Ryrie. *Caddie Woodlawn*. Trina Schart Hyman, illustrator. New York: Macmillan, 1973.

Brown, Marcia. *Shadow*. New York: Charles Scribner's Sons, 1982.

Brown, Ruth. *A Dark, Dark Tale*. New York: Dial, 1984.

Brown, Tricia. *Hello Amigos!* Frank Ortiz, illustrator. New York: Henry Holt, 1986.

Burch, Robert. *Queenie Peavy*. Jerry Lazare, illustrator. New York: Viking, 1966.

Burnett, Frances Hodgson. *The Secret Garden*. Tasha Tudor, illustrator. Philadelphia: Lippincott, 1962.

Burningham, John. *John Patrick Norman McHennessy — The Boy Who Was Always Late*. New York: Crown, 1987.

Butler, Beverly. *Ghost Cat*. New York: Dodd Mead, 1984.

Byars, Betsy. *The Eighteenth Emergency*. Robert Grossman, illustrator. New York: Viking, 1973.

————. *Trouble River*. New York: Viking, 1971.

Calhoun, May. *Julie's Tree*. New York: Harper and Row, 1988.

Cleary, Beverly. *Dear Mr. Henshaw*. Paul O. Zelinsky, illustrator. New York: William Morrow, 1983.

Cleaver, Elizabeth. *The Enchanted Caribou*. New York: Atheneum, 1985.

Clifton, Lucille. *Sonora Beautiful*. Michael Garland, illustrator. New York: E. P. Dutton, 1981.

Climo, Shirley. *The Cobweb Christmas*. Joe Lasker, illustrator. New York: Thomas Y. Crowell, 1982.

Coatsworth, Emerson and David. *The Adventures of Nanabush: Ojibway Indian Stories*. Francis Kagige, illustrator. New York: Atheneum, 1980.

Coerr, Eleanor. *The Josefina Quilt Story*. Bruce Degen, illustrator. New York: Harper and Row, 1986.

Cohen, Barbara. *Thank You Jackie Robinson*. Richard Cuffari, illustrator. New York: Lothrop, Lee and Shepard, 1974.

Cohen, Caron Lee. *Sally Ann Thunder Ann Whirlwind Crockett*. Ariane Dewey, illustrator. New York: Greenwillow, 1985.

Conrad, Pam. *Prairie Songs*. Darryl S. Zudeck, illustrator. New York: Harper and Row, 1985.

Corcoran, Barbara. *I Am the Universe*. New York: Atheneum, 1986.

Denman, Cherry. *The Little Peacock's Gift*. New York: Bedrick/Blackie, 1987.

de Paola, Tomie. *The Art Lesson*. New York: G.P. Putnam's Sons, 1989.

_____. *Fin M'Coul: The Giant of Knockmany Hill*. New York: Holiday House, 1981.

_____. *The Hunter and the Animals: A Wordless Picture Book*. New York: Holiday House, 1981.

_____. *The Legend of Old Befana*. New York: Harcourt, 1980.

_____. *The Legend of the Bluebonnet: The Old Tale of Texas*. New York: G.P. Putnam's Sons, 1983.

_____. *The Legend of the Indian Paintbrush*. New York: G.P. Putnam's Sons, 1988.

_____. *Strega Nona*. Englewood Cliffs, N.J.: Prentice-Hall, 1975.

Dewey, Ariane. *Febold Feboldson*. New York: Greenwillow, 1984.

_____. *Lafitte the Pirate*. New York: Greenwillow, 1985.

_____. *Pecos Bill*. New York: Greenwillow, 1983.

Dupasquier, Phillipe. *Dear Daddy*. New York: Bradbury, 1985.

Esbensen, Barbara Juster. *Words with Wrinkled Knees: Animal Poems*. John Stadler, illustrator. New York: Thomas Y. Crowell, 1986.

Estes, Eleanor. *The Hundred Dresses*. Lois Slobodkin, illustrator. New York: Harcourt, 1944.

Fitzhugh, Louise. *Harriet the Spy*. New York: Harper and Row, 1964.

Flourney, Valerie. *The Patchwork Quilt*. Jerry Pinkney, illustrator. New York: Dial, 1985.

Fox, Mem. *Hattie and the Fox*. Patricia Mullins, illustrator. New York: Bradbury, 1987.

Fox, Paula. *The Moonlight Man*. New York: Bradbury, 1986.

––––––. *One-Eyed Cat*. New York: Bradbury, 1984.

Fritz, Jean. *China Homecoming*. Michael Fritz, photographer. New York: G.P. Putnam's Sons, 1985.

––––––. *Homesick: My Own Story*. New York: G.P. Putnam's Sons, 1982.

Froman, Robert. *Seeing Things: A Book of Poems*. New York: Thomas Y. Crowell, 1974.

––––––. *Street Poems*. New York: McCall, 1971.

Gabhart, Ann. *The Gifting*. Toronto: Crosswinds, 1987.

Galdone, Paul. *The Gingerbread Boy*. New York: Seabury, 1975.

––––––. *Henny Penny*. New York: Clarion, 1968.

––––––. *Three Aesop Fox Fables*. New York: Seabury, 1971.

––––––. *What's in Fox's Sack?* New York: Clarion, 1982.

Gammell, Stephen. *Once upon MacDonald's Farm*. New York: Four Winds Press, 1981.

Gardiner, John. *Stone Fox*. Marcia Sewall, illustrator. New York: Harper and Row, 1980.

George, Jean Craighead. *My Side of the Mountain*. New York: E.P. Dutton, 1959.

––––––. *The Talking Earth*. New York: Harper and Row, 1980.

Goble, Paul. *The Girl Who Loved Wild Horses*. New York: Bradbury, 1978.

––––––. *Iktomi and the Berries*. New York: Bradbury, 1989.

––––––. *Iktomi and the Boulder*. New York: Bradbury, 1988.

––––––. *Star Boy*. New York: Bradbury, 1983.

Godden, Rumer. *The Rocking Horse Secret*. Juliet S. Smith, illustrator. New York: Viking, 1978.

Goodall, John. *Above and Below Stairs*. New York: Atheneum, 1983.

Haeseky, Dennis. *My Father Doesn't Know about the Woods and Me*. Michael Hays, illustrator. New York: Atheneum, 1988.

Hague, Kathleen. *The Legend of the Veery Bird*. Michael Hague, illustrator. San Diego: Harcourt Brace Jovanovich, 1985.

Hall, Donald. *Oxcart Man*. Barbara Cooney, illustrator. New York: Viking, 1979.

Halvorson, Marilyn. *Nobody Said It Would Be Easy*. Toronto: Irwin, 1987.

Harris, Christie. *Mouse Woman and the Mischief-Makers*. Douglas Tait, illustrator. Toronto: McClelland and Stewart, 1977.

_____. *Mouse Woman and the Vanished Princess*. Douglas Tait, illustrator. Toronto: McClelland and Stewart, 1976.

Harvey, Brett. *My Prairie Year: Based on the Diary of Elenore Plaisted*. Deborah Kogan Ray, illustrator. New York: Holiday House, 1986.

Haviland, Virginia, editor. *North American Legends*. Ann Strugnell, illustrator. New York: Collins, 1979.

Havill, Juanita. *It Always Happens to Leona*. Emily McCully, illustrator. New York: Crown, 1989.

Heslewood, Juliet, reteller. *Legends of Earth, Air, Fire and Water*. Tamara Capellaro, Alyson MacNeil, Jane Lydbury, and Hugh Marshall, illustrators. New York: Oxford, 1989.

Hoguet, Susan Ramsey. *Solomon Grundy*. New York: E.P. Dutton, 1986.

Holman, Felice. *Slake's Limbo*. New York: Charles Scribner's Sons, 1974.

Houston, James. *Black Diamonds: A Search for Arctic Treasure*. New York: Atheneum, 1982.

_____. *Frozen Fire*. New York: Atheneum, 1977.

_____. *Wolf Run: A Caribou Eskimo Tale*. Don Mills, Ont.: Longmans, 1971.

Hudson, Jan. *Dawn Rider*. New York: Philomel, 1990.

_____. *Sweetgrass*. Edmonton, Alberta: Treefrog Press, 1984.

Hughes, Monica. *The Dream Catcher*. Toronto: Methuen, 1986.

_____. *Hunter in the Dark*. Toronto: Avon, 1984.

Hutchins, Pat. *Rosie's Walk*. New York: Macmillan, 1968.

Isadora, Rachel. *Willaby*. New York: Macmillan, 1977.

Keats, Ezra Jack. *Little Drummer Boy*. Words and Music by K. Davis and H. Onorati and H. Simeone. New York: Macmillan, 1968.

Keith, Harold. *The Obstinate Land*. New York: Thomas Y. Crowell, 1977.

Kellogg, Steven. *Johnny Appleseed: A Tall Tale*. New York: William Morrow, 1988.

_____. *The Mystery of the Magic Green Ball*. New York: Dial, 1978.

_____. *The Mystery of the Missing Red Mitten*. New York: Dial, 1974.

_____. *Paul Bunyan*. New York: William Morrow, 1984.

Khalsa, Dayal Kaur. *Tales of a Gambling Grandma*. New York: Clarkson Potter, 1986.

Kimmelman, Leslie. *Frannie's Fruits*. Petra Mathers, illustrator. New York: Harper and Row, 1989.

Kiser, Su Ann and Kevin. *The Birthday Thing*. Yassi Abolafia, illustrator. New York: Atheneum, 1987.

Konigsburg, Elaine. *From the Mixed-up Files of Mrs. Basil E. Frankweiler*. New York: Atheneum, 1967.

Krahn, Fernando. *The Mystery of Giant Footprints*. New York: E.P. Dutton, 1977.

Kroeber, Theodora. *Ishi, Last of His Tribe*. Ruth Robbins, illustrator. Toronto: Bantam, 1964.

Kurelek, William. *Prairie Boy's Summer*. Montreal: Tundra Books, 1975.

_____. *Prairie Boy's Winter*. Montreal: Tundra Books, 1975.

Lampman, Evelyn Sibley. *Potlatch Family*. New York: Atheneum, 1976.

Lee, Jeanne M. *The Legend of Li River*. New York: Holt, Rinehart & Winston, 1983.

_____. *Legend of the Milky Way*. New York: Holt, Rinehart & Winston, 1982.

Lester, Julius. *The Tales of Uncle Remus: the Adventures of Brer Rabbit*. Jerry Pinkney, illustrator. New York: Dial, 1987.

Lewis, C.S. *The Lion, the Witch and the Wardrobe*. Pauline Baynes, illustrator. New York: Macmillan, 1968.

Lionni, Leo. "Tico and the Golden Wings" in *Frederick's Fables: A Leo Lionni Treasury of Favorite Stories*. New York: Pantheon, 1985.

Little, Jean. *Different Dragons*. Laura Fernandez, illustrator. Toronto: Penguin, 1986.

_____. *From Anna*. Joan Sandin, illustrator. New York: Harper and Row, 1972.

_____. *Mama's Going to Buy You a Mockingbird*. Toronto: Penguin, 1984.

Livingston, Myra Cohn. *Sky Songs*. Leonard Everett Fisher. New York: Holiday House, 1984.

Lobe, Mira. *The Snowman Who Went for a Walk*. Winfried Opgenoorth. New York: William Morrow, 1984.

Lord, Betty Bao. *In the Year of the Boar and Jackie Robinson*. Marc Simant, illustrator. New York: Harper and Row, 1984.

Lowry, Lois. *Anastasia Has the Answers*. New York: Houghton Mifflin, 1986.

Lunn, Janet. *The Root Cellar*. Toronto: Lester and Orpen Dennys, 1983.

Lyon, George Ella. *Father Time and the Day Boxes*. Robert Andrew Parker, illustrator. New York: Bradbury, 1985.

Macaulay, David. *Why the Chicken Crossed the Road*. New York: Houghton Mifflin, 1987.

Major, Kevin. *Hold Fast*. Toronto: Clarke Irwin, 1978.

Martin, Ann M. *Ten Kids No Pets*. New York: Holiday House, 1988.

Mathis, Sharon Bell. *The Hundred Penny Box*. Leo and Diane Dillon, illustrators. New York: Viking, 1975.

Mayer, Marianna. *Aladdin and the Enchanted Lamp*. Gerald McDermott, illustrator. New York: Macmillan, 1985.

Mazer, Norma Fox. *After the Rain*. New York: William Morrow, 1987.

McDermott, Gerald. *Daniel O'Rourke*. New York: Viking, 1986.

McHargue, Georges. *Funny Bananas: The Mystery at the Museum*. Heidi Palmer, illustrator. New York: Holt, 1975.

McKissack, Patricia C. *Flossie and the Fox*. Rachel Isadora, illustrator. New York: Dial, 1986.

Miles, Bernard. *Robin Hood: His Life and Legend*. Victor Ambrus, illustrator. New York: Hamlyn, 1979.

Miles, Miska. *Annie and the Old One*. Peter Parnall, illustrator. New York: Little, Brown, 1971.

Mikolaycak, Charles, reteller. *Babushka*. New York: Holiday House, 1984.

Mowat, Farley. *Lost in the Barrens*. Charles Geer, illustrator. Toronto: McClelland and Stewart, 1966.

Ness, Evaline. *Sam, Bangs and Moonshine*. New York: Holt, Rinehart, 1968.

Noble, Trinka Hakes. *Meanwhile Back at the Ranch*. Tony Ross, illustrator. New York: Dial, 1987.

_____. *The Day Jimmy's Boa Ate the Wash*. Steven Kellogg, illustrator. New York: Dial, 1980.

Norton, Juster. *As: A Surfeit of Similes*. David Small, illustrator. New York: William Morrow, 1989.

O'Dell, Scott. *Island of the Blue Dolphins*. New York: Houghton Mifflin, 1960.

_____. *Zia*. New York: Laurel Leaf, 1976.

O'Kelley, Mattie Lou. *From the Hills of Georgia: An Autobiography in Paintings*. Boston: Atlantic Monthly Press Books, 1983.

Park, Barbara. *Almost Starring Skinnybones*. New York: Knopf, 1988.

_____. *Skinnybones*. New York: Knopf, 1982.

Parnall, Peter. *Quiet*. New York: Morrow Junior Books, 1989.

Paterson, Katherine. *Bridge to Terabithia*. Donna Diamond, illustrator. New York: Thomas Y. Crowell, 1977.

_____. *The Great Gilly Hopkins*. New York: Thomas Y. Crowell, 1978.

_____. *Jacob Have I Loved*. New York: Thomas Y. Crowell, 1980.

Paulsen, Gary. *Hatchet*. New York: Bradbury, 1987.

Pearce, Philippa. *The Way to Sattin Shore*. Charlotte Voake, illustrator. New York: Greenwillow, 1983.

Pelly, Linda. *Saulteaux Legends (Nanabush)*. Ray McCallum and Larry Okanee, illustrators. Saskatoon: Saskatchewan Indian Cultural College, 1981.

Pelowski, Anne. *Winding Valley Farm: Annie's Story*. Wendy Watson, illustrator. New York: Philomel, 1982.

Pendergraf, Patricia. *Hear the Wind Blow*. New York: Philomel, 1968.

Philip, Neil. *The Tale of Sir Gawain*. Charles Keeping, illustrator. New York: Philomel, 1987.

Polacco, Patricia. *The Keeping Quilt*. New York: Simon and Schuster, 1988.

Potter, Beatrix. *The Tale of Peter Rabbit*. London: Frederick Warne, 1902.

Quinlan, Patricia. *Anna's Red Sled*. Lindsay Grater, illustrator. Toronto: Annick, 1989.

Raskin, Ellen. *The Mysterious Disappearance of Leon (I Mean Noel)*. New York: E.P. Dutton, 1971.

_____. *The Westing Game*. New York: E.P. Dutton, 1976.

Renberg, Dalia Hardof. *Hello, Clouds!* Alona Frankel, illustrator. New York: Harper and Row, 1985.

Reynolds, Kathy. *Marco Polo*. Daniel Woods, illustrator. Milwaukee, WI: Raintree, 1986.

Riordan, James. *Tales of King Arthur*. Victor Ambrus, illustrator. New York: Rand McNally, 1982.

Robinson, Gail. *Raven, the Trickster: Legends of the North American Indians*. Joanna Troughton, illustrator. New York: Atheneum, 1982.

Robinson, Ruth. *Taliesan and King Arthur*. New York: Parnassus, 1970.

Ross, Tony. *I'm Coming to Get You*. New York: Dial, 1984.

_____. *Stone Soup*. New York: Dial, 1987.

Roth, Susan. *The Patchwork Tales*. Ruth Phang, illustrator. New York: Atheneum, 1981.

Rounds, Glen. *The Morning the Sun Refused to Shine*. New York: Holiday House, 1984.

_____. *Washday on Noah's Ark*. New York: Holiday House, 1985.

Rylant, Cynthia. *A Fine White Dust*. New York: Bradbury, 1986.

_____. *Waiting to Waltz: A Childhood*. Stephen Gammell, illustrator. New York: Bradbury, 1984.

_____. *When I Was Young in the Mountains*. New York: E.P. Dutton, 1982.

Sachs, Marilyn. *Fran Ellen's House*. New York: E.P. Dutton, 1987.

Sadler, Marilyn. *Alistair's Elephant*. Roger Bollen. Englewood Cliffs, N.J.: Prentice-Hall, 1983.

Sancha, Sheila. *The Luttrell Village: Country Life in the Middle Ages*. New York: Thomas Y. Crowell, 1983.

San Souci, Robert. *The Legend of Scarface: A Blackfeet Indian Tale*. Daniel San Souci, illustrator. New York: Doubleday, 1978.

_____. *The Talking Eggs*. Jerry Pinkney, illustrator. New York: Dial, 1989.

Scieszka, Jon. *The True Story of the 3 Little Pigs by A. Wolf*. Lane Smith, illustrator. New York: Viking, 1989.

Scribe, Murdo. *Murdo's Story: A Legend from Northern Manitoba*. Terry Gallagher, illustrator. Winnipeg: Pemmican, 1985.

Sharmat, Marjorie Weiman. *The 329th Friend*. Cyndy Szekeres, illustrator. New York: Four Winds Press, 1979.

Sherlock, Phillip. *Anansi the Spider Man: Jamaican Folk Tales*. Marcia Brown, illustrator. New York: Thomas Y. Crowell, 1954.

Sherman, Ivan. *Walking Talking Words*. San Diego: Harcourt Brace Jovanovich, 1980.

Shute, Linda. *Clever Tom and the Leprechaun: An Old Irish Story*. New York: Lothrop, Lee and Shepard, 1988.

Silverstein, Shel. *Who Wants a Cheap Rhinoceros?* New York: Macmillan, 1983.

Slobodkin, Esphyr. *Caps for Sale*. New York: Addison Wesley, 1947.

Smucker, Barbara. *White Mist*. Toronto: Irwin, 1987.

Snyder, Dianne. *The Boy of the Three-Year Nap*. Allen Say, illustrator. New York: Houghton Mifflin, 1988.

Spalding, Andrea. *The Most Beautiful Kite in the World*. Georgia Graham, illustrator. Red Deer, Alberta: Red Deer College Press, 1988.

Steig, William. *Doctor DeSoto*. New York: Farrar, Straus and Giroux, 1982.

Steptoe, John. *The Story of Jumping Mouse*. New York: Lothrop, Lee and Shepard, 1984.

Stevenson, James. *We Hate Rain!* New York: Greenwillow, 1985.

————. *What's under My Bed?* New York: Greenwillow, 1983.

Sturton, Hugh. *Zomo the Rabbit*. Peter Warner, illustrator. New York: Atheneum, 1966.

Taylor, Cora. *Julie*. Saskatoon: Western Producer Prairie Books, 1985.

Taylor, Mildred. *Roll of Thunder, Hear Me Cry*. New York: Dial, 1976.

Toye, William. *The Loon's Necklace*. Elizabeth Cleaver, illustrator. Toronto: Oxford, 1977.

————. *The Mountain Goats of Temlaham*. Elizabeth Cleaver, illustrator. Toronto: Oxford, 1969.

Turkel, Brinton. *Deep in the Forest*. New York: E.P. Dutton, 1976.

Van Allsburg, Chris. *The Garden of Abdul Gasazi*. New York: Houghton Mifflin, 1979.

————. *The Mysteries of Harris Burdick*. New York: Houghton Mifflin, 1984.

Viorst, Judith. *The Good-Bye Book*. Kay Chorao, illustrator. New York: Atheneum, 1988.

Voight, Cynthia. *Dicey's Song*. New York: Atheneum, 1982.

Wagner, Jenny. *John Brown, Rose and the Midnight Cat*. Ron Brooks, illustrator. New York: Bradbury, 1978.

Wallace, Ian. *The Sparrow's Song*. Toronto: Penguin, 1986.

Wason-Ellam, Linda. *The Legend of Calgary*. Calgary, Alberta: Warren West Ltd., 1987.

Waterton, Betty. *Pettranella*. Ann Blades, illustrator. Vancouver: Douglas and McIntyre, 1980.

Weil, Lisl. *I, Christopher Columbus*. New York: Atheneum, 1983.

Weiss, Jacqueline Shachter. *Young Brer Rabbit, and Other Trickster Tales from the Americas*. Clinton Arrowwood, illustrator. Baltimore: Stemmer House/Barbara Holdridge Books, 1985.

West, Colin. *The King of Kennelwick Castle*. Anne Dalton, illustrator. Philadelphia: Lippincott, 1986.

Westwood, Jennifer. *Going to Squintum's: A Foxy Folktale*. Fiona French, illustrator. New York: Dial, 1985.

Williams, Jay. *Everyone Knows What a Dragon Looks Like*. Mercer Mayer, illustrator. New York: Four Winds Press, 1976.

Williams, Margery. *The Velveteen Rabbit*. William Nicholson, illustrator. New York: Doubleday, 1958 (1922).

Williams, Vera. *Something Special for Me*. New York: Greenwillow, 1983.

_____. *Three Days on a River in a Red Canoe*. New York: Greenwillow, 1981.

Wrightson, Patricia. *Moon-Dad*. Noella Young, illustrator. New York: Atheneum, 1987.

Yashima, Taro. *Crow Boy*. New York: Viking, 1955.

Yates, Elizabeth. *My Diary — My World*. Philadelphia: Westminster Press, 1981.

Yolen, Jane. *Owl Moon*. John Schoenherr, illustrator. New York: Philomel, 1987.

_____. ''Silent Bianca'', in *The Girl Who Cried Flowers*. New York: Thomas Y. Crowell, 1974.

Zemach, Margot. *It Could Always Be Worse: A Yiddish Folk Tale*. New York: Farrar, Straus and Giroux, 1976.

Wordless Picture Books for Beginning Students

Alexander, Martha. *Bobo's Dream*. New York: Dial, 1970. A daschund loses his bone to a larger dog. When he dreams, he becomes a larger than life-sized hero and rescues his master's football.

Aruego, Jose. *Look What I Can Do*. New York: Charles Scribner's Sons, 1971. Two caribous cavort while other animals watch. When they are exhausted by their activities, a third caribou enters.

Bang, Molly. *The Grey Lady and the Strawberry Snatcher*. New York: Four Winds Press, 1980. A blue monster chases an old lady.

Briggs, Raymond. *The Snowman*. London: Penguin, 1978. A snowman comes to life and adventures through a strange world.

Burningham, John. *Seasons*. Indianapolis: Bobbs-Merrill, 1970. The cycle of the seasons is captured in full-color scenes.

Carle, Eric. *Do You Want to Be My Friend?* New York: Thomas Y. Crowell, 1971. A little mouse is looking for a friend but all the other animals are too busy. The mouse asks the horse, then in turn an alligator, a lion, a hippo, a seal, a monkey, a peacock, a fox, a kangaroo, a giraffe, and a snake.

Carroll, Ruth. *Rolling Downhill*. New York: Walck, 1973. A dog and a cat become entangled in a ball of yarn.

_____. *What Whiskers Did*. New York: Walck, 1965. A puppy breaks his leash. He follows a rabbit into its hole to avoid a fox.

Crewes, Donald. *Truck*. New York: Greenwillow, 1978. A red truck weaves in and out of traffic.

de Paola, Tomie. *Pancakes for Breakfast*. San Diego: Harcourt Brace and Jovanovich, 1978. A woman searches for ingredients to make her pancakes from a cow and a hen and others.

Dresher, Henrik. *The Yellow Umbrella*. New York: Bradbury, 1987. Two monkeys find adventure when they retrieve a yellow umbrella.

Goodall, John S. *Little Red Riding Hood*. New York: Atheneum, 1988. A retelling of the classic with a mouse as the main character.

Hogrogian, Nonny. *Apples*. New York: Macmillan, 1972. A little boy throws away an apple core. Many other animals leave their cores until an orchard grows.

Krahn, Fernando. *The Self-Made Snowman*. Philadelphia: Lippincott, 1974. A snowman is made from an avalanche in the mountains.

144

_____. *Who's Seen Scissors*. New York: E. P. Dutton, 1975. A tailor's scissors cut through newspapers, a clothesline, and instrument strings among other things before they are returned and put in a cage by the tailor.

Prater, John. *The Gift*. New York: Viking, 1987. Two young children have a marvelous adventure when they jump inside a mysterious package.

Ringi, Kjell. *The Magic Stick*. New York: Harper and Row, 1968. A boy picks up a magic stick that becomes a magician's wand, riding whip, spyglass, and sword. He throws away the stick when other children laugh at him.

Sasaki, Isao. *Snow*. New York: Viking, 1982. Thick fluffy snow makes a soft and silent world at a railroad station. The arrival and departure of a train breaks the quietness of the day.

Schick, Emma. *Making Friends*. New York: Macmillan, 1968. A little child offers friendship to a host of story animals until he finally meets another child.

Shimin, Symeon. *A Special Birthday*. New York: McGraw Hill, 1976. A little girl wakes to find a ball of ribbon on her pillow. She follows the ribbon until she finds her wrapped birthday presents.

Spier, Peter. *Dreams*. New York: Doubleday, 1986. A boy and a girl imagine strange and wonderful shapes as they watch clouds drift by.

_____. *Peter Spier's Christmas!* New York: Doubleday, 1983. A family is followed through the festivities of Christmas.

_____. *Peter Spier's Rain*. New York: Doubleday, 1982. The adventures of two children as they explore the world on a rainy day.

Turkel, Brinton. *Deep in the Forest*. New York: E.P. Dutton, 1985. A little bear invades a house while the family is not home in this reversal of *Goldilocks and the Three Bears*.

Ueno, Noriko. *Elephant Buttons*. New York: Harper and Row, 1973. The elephant unbuttons himself, and out steps a horse who unbuttons himself and out steps a lion. Then in turn a seal, monkey, duck, and mouse appear.

Ungerer, Tomi. *One, Two, Where's My Shoe*. New York: Harper and Row, 1964. The shoe form is seen as a bird, ship, fish, snakes, etc.

_____. *Snail, Where Are You?* New York: Harper and Row, 1962.

A repeated snail design is seen as a tuba, waves, horns, smoke rings, and a pig's tail.

Young, Ed. *The Other Bone*. New York: Harper and Row, 1983. A dog loses his bone when it splashes into a pond. A variation on Aesop's *The Dog and the Bone*.

———. *Up a Tree*. New York: Harper and Row, 1983. A cat climbs up a tree after being chased by a dog.

Wordless Books for Developing Students

Anno, Mitsumasa. *Anno's Britain*. New York: Philomel, 1982. An illustrated journey through Great Britain.

———. *Anno's Flea Market*. London: Bodley Head, 1984. Illustrations follow a viewer through a flea market in a European city.

———. *Anno's Italy*. Don Mills: Collins, 1980. A traveler is followed throughout Italy in colorful illustrations.

———. *Anno's Journey*. New York: Philomel, 1978. An artist's journey through the villages and cities of Europe.

Charlip, Remy, and Jerry Joyner. *Thirteen*. New York: Parents, 1975. Thirteen simultaneous stories are unfolded simultaneously. Very creative format.

Fuchs, Erich. *Journey to the Moon*. New York: Delacorte, 1969. An eight-day mission aboard Apollo II.

Goodall, John S. *Story of Main Street*. New York: Atheneum, 1987. An ever-changing scene of an English market centre from medieval times to the present day.

———. *The Story of a Castle*. New York: Atheneum, 1986. The uses of a medieval castle.

———. *The Story of an English Village*. San Diego: Harcourt Brace and Jovanovich, 1979. The changes in an English village over several centuries.

Van Allsburg, Chris. *The Mysteries of Harris Burdick*. New York: Houghton Mifflin, 1984. (Almost wordless.) Surrealistic pictures create mysterious plots for a reader's fantasies.

Ward, Lynd. *The Silver Pony*. New York: Hougton Mifflin, 1974. The adventures of a boy and a silver pony.

Wiesner, David. *Free Fall*. New York: Lothrop, Lee and Shepard, 1988. A young boy goes to a fantasy land in his dreams.

Chapter 5: Art

Aardema, Verna. *Bringing the Rain to Kapiti Plain*. Beatriz Vidal, illustrator. New York: Dial, 1981.

———. *Why Mosquitoes Buzz in People's Ears*. Leo and Diane Dillon, illustrators. New York: Dial, 1975.

Adams, Pam. *There Were Ten in the Bed*. London: Child's Play, 1985.

Aesop. *Aesop's Fables*. Heidi Holder, illustrator. New York: Viking, 1981.

Aliki. *How a Book Is Made*. New York: Thomas Y. Crowell, 1986.

Anno, Mitsumasa. *Anno's Alphabet: An Adventure in Imagination*. New York: Thomas Y. Crowell, 1975.

———. *Anno's Flea Market*. London: Bodley Head, 1984.

———. *Anno's Journey*. New York: Collins, 1978.

———. *Anno's Sundial*. New York: Philomel, 1985.

Aruego, José, and Ariane Dewey. *We Hide, You Seek*. New York: Greenwillow, 1979.

Baker, Jeannie. *Home in the Sky*. New York: Greenwillow, 1984.

———. *Where the Forest Meets the Sea*. New York: Greenwillow, 1989.

Bang, Molly. *The Paper Crane*. New York: Greenwillow, 1985.

———. *Ten, Nine, Eight*. New York: Greenwillow, 1983.

Berger, Barbara. *Gwinna*. New York: Philomel, 1990.

Bible. *Christmas: The King James Version*. Jan Piénkowski, illustrator. New York: Knopf, 1984.

Birrer, Cynthia and William, retellers. *The Shoemaker and the Elves*. New York: Lothrop, Lee and Shepard, 1983.

Brett, Jan. *Goldilocks and the Three Bears*. New York: Dodd, Mead, 1987.

———. *The Wild Christmas Reindeer*. New York: G.P. Putnam's Sons, 1990.

Brown, Marcia. *Shadow*. New York: Charles Scribner's Sons, 1982.

Bryan, Ashley. *Lion and the Ostrich Chicks and Other African Folk Tales*. New York: Atheneum, 1986.

Bunting, Eve. *Scary, Scary Halloween*. Jan Brett, illustrator. New York: Tichnor and Fields, 1986.

Carle, Eric. *The Tiny Seed*. Saxonville, MA: Picture Book Studio, 1987.

————. *The Very Busy Spider*. New York: G. P. Putnam's Sons, 1985.

————. *The Very Quiet Cricket*. New York: Philomel, 1990.

Carter, David. *Surprise Party*. New York: Grosset and Dunlap, 1990.

Cauley, Lorinda Bryan, reteller. *Jack and the Beanstalk*. New York: G. P. Putnam's Sons, 1983.

Chase, Edith. *The New Baby Calf*. Barbara Reid, illustrator. Richmond Hill, Ontario: Scholastic-Tab, 1984.

Cheng, Hou'tien. *Six Chinese Brothers*. New York: Holt, Rinehart and Winston, 1979.

Clymer, Eleanor. *Horatio Goes to the Country*. Robert Quakenbush, illustrator. New York: Macmillan, 1974.

Collins, Meghan. *The Willow Maiden*. Laszlo Gal, illustrator. New York: Dial, 1988.

Conover, Chris. *Mother Goose and the Sly Fox*. New York: Farrar, Straus and Giroux, 1989.

Cooney, Barbara (adapting from Geoffrey Chaucer). *Chanticleer and the Fox*. New York: Thomas Y. Crowell, 1958.

Craig, Helen. *Mouse House Months*. New York: Random House, 1981.

Cross, Peter. *Trouble for Trumpets*. New York: Random House, 1984.

Crowther, Robert. *The Most Amazing Hide-and-Seek Alphabet Book*. New York: Viking, 1978.

————. *The Most Amazing Hide-and-Seek Counting Book*. New York: Viking, 1981.

De Armond, Dale. *Berry Woman's Children*. New York: Greenwillow, 1985.

de Paola, Tomie. *Georgio's Village*. New York: G. P. Putnam's Sons, 1982.

Dewey, Ariane. *The Thunder God's Son*. New York: Greenwillow, 1981.

Duff, Maggie. *Dancing Turtle*. Maria Horvath, illustrator. New York: Macmillan, 1981.

Ehlert, Lois. *Color Zoo*. New York: Harper, 1989.

Eisen, Armand. *Goldilocks and the Three Bears*. Lynn Bywaters Ferris, illustrator. New York: Knopf, 1987.

Frost, Robert. *Stopping by Woods on a Snowy Evening*. Susan Jeffers, illustrator. New York: E. P. Dutton, 1978.

Gale, Don. *Sooshewan Child of the Beothuk*. Shawn Steffler, illustrator. St. John's, Nfld.: Breakwater Books, 1988.

Gay, Marie Louise. *Moonbeam on a Cat's Ear*. Toronto: Stoddart, 1986.

Goble, Paul. *Buffalo Woman*. New York: Bradbury, 1984.

_____. *The Girl Who Loved Wild Horses*. New York: Bradbury, 1978.

Godden, Rumer. *The Dragon of Og*. Pauline Baynes, illustrator. New York: Viking, 1981.

Goodall, John. *Luvinia's Cottage*. New York: Atheneum, 1983.

_____. *Shrewbettina Goes to Work*. New York: Atheneum, 1981.

Hague, Michael, compiler. *Aesop's Fables*. Illustrated by the compiler. New York: Holt, Rinehart and Winston, 1985.

Harris, Rosemary, reteller. *Beauty and the Beast*. Errol LeCain, illustrator. New York: Doubleday, 1979.

Harrison, Ted. *The Northern Alphabet*. Montreal: Tundra, 1977.

Heyer, Marilee. *The Weaving of a Dream: A Chinese Folktale*. New York: Viking, 1986.

Hodges, Margaret, reteller. *St. George and the Dragon*. Trina Schart Hyman, illustrator. New York: Little, Brown, 1984.

Hogrogian, Nonny. *The Glass Mountain: Retold from the Tale by the Brothers Grimm*. Illustrated by the author. New York: Knopf, 1985.

Hutchins, Pat. *Changes, Changes*. New York: Macmillan, 1971.

_____. *One Hunter*. New York: Greenwillow, 1982.

_____. *The Surprise Party*. New York: Macmillan, 1969.

Hyman, Trina Schart. *Little Red Riding Hood*. New York: Holiday House, 1983.

Isele, Elizabeth. *The Frog Princess*. Michael Hague, illustrator. New York: Thomas Y. Crowell, 1984.

Jonas, Ann. *Color Dance*. New York: Greenwillow, 1989.

_____. *Reflections*. New York: Greenwillow, 1987.

Kennedy, Richard. *Song of the Horse*. Marcia Sewall, illustrator. New York: Unicorn, 1981.

Lang, Andrew. *Aladdin and the Wonderful Lamp*. Errol LeCain, illustrator. New York: Viking, 1981.

Laroche, Michel. *The Snow Rose*. Sandra Laroche, illustrator. New York: Holiday House, 1986.

Lenski, Lois. *Sing a Song of People*. Giles Laroche, illustrator. New York: Little, Brown, 1987.

Lent, Blair. *Baybury Bluff*. New York: Houghton Mifflin, 1987.

Lionni, Leo. *Frederick*. New York: Pantheon, 1967.

_____. *Let's Make Rabbits*. New York: Pantheon, 1982.

_____. *Swimmy*. New York: Pantheon, 1963.

_____. "Tico and the Golden Wings", in *Frederick Fables: A Leo Lionni Treasury of Favorite Stories*. New York: Pantheon, 1985.

Lobe, Mira. *The Snowman Who Went for a Walk*. Winfried Opgenoorth, illustrator. New York: William Morrow, 1984.

Longfellow, Henry Wadsworth. *Hiawatha's Childhood*. Errol LeCain, illustrator. New York: Farrar Strauss, 1984.

MacCarthy, Patricia. *Animals Galore*. New York: Dial, 1989.

Macaulay, David. *Castle*. New York: Houghton Mifflin, 1977.

_____. *Cathedral: The Story of Its Construction*. New York: Houghton Mifflin, 1973.

_____. *City: A Story of Roman Planning and Construction*. New York: Hougton Mifflin, 1974.

_____. *Pyramid*. New York: Houghton Mifflin, 1975.

Mahy, Margaret. *17 Kings and 42 Elephants*. Patricia MacCarthy, illustrator. New York: Dial, 1987.

Marshall, Ray. *The Plane*. John Bradley, illustrator. New York: Viking, 1985.

Martin, Eva. *Canadian Fairy Tales*. Laszlo Gal, illustrator. Vancouver: Douglas and McIntyre, 1984.

McClain, Mary, illustrator. *Hansel and Gretel: A Peepshow Book*. Toronto: Clarke, Irwin and Co., 1975.

McDermott, Gerald. *Anansi, the Spider: A Tale from the Ashanti*. New York: Holt, Rinehart and Winston, 1972.

_____. *Arrow to the Sun: A Pueblo Indian Tale*. New York: Viking, 1974.

McLerran, Alice. *The Mountain That Loved a Bird*. Eric Carle, illustrator. Saxonville, MA: Picture Book Studio, 1985.

Mikolaycak, Charles, reteller and illustrator. *Babushka*. New York: Holiday House, 1984.

Miller, Jonathan. *The Human Body*. David Pelham, illustrator. New York: Viking, 1983.

Narahashi, Keiko. *I Have a Friend*. New York: Macmillan, 1987.

Oppenheim, Joanne. *Have You Seen Birds?* Barbara Reid, illustrator. Richmond Hill, Ontario: Scholastic-Tab, 1986.

Perrault, Charles. *The Sleeping Beauty*. David Walker, illustrator. New York: Thomas Y. Crowell, 1976.

Peters, David. *Giants of the Land, Sea and Air: Past and Present*. New York: Knopf, 1986.

Peveor, Richard. *Mister Cat-and-a-Half*. Robert Ravensky, illustrator. New York: Macmillan, 1986.

Pienkowski, Jan. *Gossip*. London: Gallery Five, 1983.

_____. *Haunted House*. New York: E. P. Dutton, 1979.

Pomerantz, Charolotte. *One Duck Another Duck*. José Aruego and Ariane Dewey, illustrators. New York: Greenwillow, 1984.

Potter, Beatrix. *The Peter Rabbit Pop-Up Book*. New York: Warne, 1983.

Prokofiev, Sergei. *Peter and the Wolf*. Barbara Cooney, illustrator. New York: Viking, 1985.

Provensen, Alice and Martin. *Leonardo da Vinci*. New York: Viking, 1984.

Radin, Ruth Yaffe. *High in the Mountains*. Ed Young, illustrator. New York: Macmillan, 1989.

Reid, Barbara. *Playing with Plasticine*. New York: William Morrow, 1989.

Reinl, Edda. *The Little Snake*. Boston: Neugenbauer Press, 1982.

Reit, Seymour. *Those Fabulous Flying Machines: A History of Flight in Three Dimensions with Punch-Out Plane Model*. Randy Weidner, illustrator. Concept by Ib Pennick and Chris Crowell. New York: Macmillan, 1985.

Robbins, Ruth. *How the First Rainbow Was Made*. New York: Parnassus, 1980.

_____. *Taliesin and King Arthur*. New York: Parnassus, 1970.

Ross, Tony. *The Three Little Pigs*. New York: Pantheon, 1983.

Russell, Naomi. *The Tree*. New York: E. P. Dutton, 1989.

Samton, Sheila White. *Beside the Bay*. New York: Philomel, 1987.

Segal, Lore. *The Story of Old Mrs. Brubeck and How She Looked for Trouble and Where She Found Him*. Marcia Sewall, illustrator. New York: Pantheon, 1981.

Service, Robert. *The Shooting of Dan McGrew*. Ted Harrison, illustrator. Toronto: Kids Can Press, 1988.

Simon, Hilda. *The Magic of Color*. New York: Lothrop, Lee and Shephard, 1981.

Tarrant, Graham. *Frogs*. Tony King, illustrator. New York: G.P. Putnam's Sons, 1983.

Tejima. *Fox's Dream.* New York: Philomel, 1987.

———. *Ho-Limlim: A Rabbit Tale from Japan.* New York: Philomel, 1990.

———. *Owl Lake.* New York: Philomel, 1987.

———. *Swan Sky.* New York: Philomel, 1988.

———. *Woodpecker Forest.* New York: Philomel, 1989.

Toye, William. *The Mountain Goats of Temlaham.* Elizabeth Cleaver, illustrator. Toronto: Oxford, 1969.

Wallner, John. *Sleeping Beauty.* New York: Viking, 1987.

———. *The Three Little Pigs.* New York: Viking, 1987.

Walsh, Ellen Stoll. *Mouse Paint.* San Diego: Harcourt, Brace and Jovanovich, 1989.

Wildsmith, Brian. *Pelican.* New York: Pantheon, 1983.

Wisniewski, David. *The Warrior and the Wiseman.* New York: Lothrop, 1989.

Wolff, Ashley. *A Year of Birds.* New York: Dodd, Mead, 1984.

Wood, John Norris. *Nature Hide and Seek: Jungles.* John Norris Wood and Kevin Dean, illustrators. New York: Knopf, 1987.

———. *Nature Hide and Seek: Oceans.* John Norris Wood and Kevin Dean, illustrators. New York: Knopf, 1988.

Yashima, Taro. *Crow Boy.* New York: Viking, 1955.

Yolen, Jane. *The Emperor and the Kite.* Ed Young, illustrator. New York: Philomel, 1988.

Young, Ed. *Lon Po Po: A Red Riding Hood Story from China.* New York: Philomel, 1989.

Zelinsky, Paul O. *Rumpelstiltskin.* New York: E.P. Dutton, 1986.

Chapter 6: Music

Aardema, Verna. *Rabbit Makes a Monkey of Lion.* Jerry Pinkney, illustrator. New York: Dial, 1989.

———. *The Vingananee and the Tree Toad: A Liberian Tale.* Ellen Weiss, illustrator. New York: Frederick Warne, 1983.

Alexander, Lloyd. *The Jedera Adventure.* New York: E. P. Dutton, 1989.

Allan, Benjamin. *Rat-a-Tat, Pitter Pat.* Margaret Miller, photographer. New York: Thomas Y. Crowell, 1987.

Baylor, Byrd. *Desert Voices.* Peter Parnall, illustrator. New York: Charles Scribner's Sons, 1981.

_____. *Hawk, I'm Your Brother*. Peter Parnall, illustrator. New York: Charles Scribner's Sons, 1976.

Brett, Jan. *The Twelve Days of Christmas*. New York: Philomel, 1990.

Carey, Valerie Scho. *Quail Song: A Pueblo Indian Tale*. New York: Putnam, 1990.

Cole, Joanna. *It's Too Noisy*. Kate Duke, illustrator. New York: Thomas Y. Crowell, 1989.

Crews, Donald. *Carousel*. New York: Greenwillow, 1982.

_____. *Parade*. New York: Greenwillow, 1983.

Duff, Maggie. *Rum Pum Pum: A Folktale from India*. José Aruego and Ariane Dewey. New York: Macmillan, 1978.

Gage, Wilson. *Down in the Boondocks*. Glen Rounds, illustrator. New York: Greenwillow, 1977.

Galdone, Paul. *The Teeny-Tiny Woman*. New York: Clarion, 1984.

_____. *The Three Billy Goats Gruff*. New York: Clarion, 1973.

Grimm Brothers. (Wesley Porter, reteller.) *The Musicians of Bremen*. Kenneth W. Mitchell, illustrator. New York: Franklin Watts, 1979.

Hasely, Dennis. *The Old Banjo*. Stephen Gammell, illustrator. New York: Macmillan, 1983.

Hastings, Selina. *Peter and the Wolf*. Reg Cartwright, illustrator. New York: Henry Holt, 1987.

Hoffmann, E.T. (Ralph Manheim, translator.) *Nutcracker*. Maurice Sendak, illustrator. New York: Crown, 1984.

Hutchins, Pat. *Good Night Owl*. New York: Macmillan, 1982.

Jeffers, Susan. *All the Pretty Little Horses*. New York: Macmillan, 1967.

Kovalski, Maryann. *The Wheels on the Bus*. Toronto: Kids Can Press, 1987.

Langstaff, John. *The Golden Vanity*. David Gentleman, illustrator. San Diego: Harcourt Brace Jovanovich, 1972.

Lee, Dennis. *Alligator Pie*. Frank Newfeld, illustrator. Toronto: Macmillan, 1974.

_____. *Garbage Delight*. Frank Newfeld, illustrator. Toronto: Macmillan, 1978.

Mosel, Arlene. *The Funny Little Woman*. Blair Lent, illustrator. New York: E. P. Dutton, 1972.

Munsch, Robert. *Love You Forever*. Shirley McGraw, illustrator. Scarborough, Ont.: Firefly, 1986.

Newton, Pam (reteller). *The Stonecutter: An Indian Folktale*. New York: Putnam/Whitebird Books, 1990.

Prelutsky, Jack. *The New Kid on the Block*. Jeanne Titherington, illustrator. New York: Greenwillow, 1984.

———. "Pumberly Pott's Unpredictable Niece" in *The Queen of Eene*. Victoria Chess, illustrator. New York: Greenwillow, 1978.

———. *Rolling Harvey Down the Hill*. Victoria Chess, illustrator. New York: Greenwillow, 1980.

Sanders, Scott. *Hear the Wind Blow: American Folksongs Retold*. Ponder Goembel, illustrator. New York: Bradbury, 1985.

Seeger, Ruth Crawford. "The Ballad of John Henry" in *American Folk Songs for Children*. Barbara Cooney, illustrator. New York: Doubleday, 1948.

Service, Robert. *The Cremation of Sam McGee*. Ted Harrison, illustrator. Toronto: Kids Can Press, 1986.

Silverstein, Shel. "The Unicorn" in *Where the Sidewalk Ends*. New York: Harper and Row, 1974.

Spier, Peter. *The Erie Canal*. New York: Doubleday, 1974.

Stanley, Diane. *Fiddle-I-Fee*. New York: Little, Brown, 1979.

Thayer, Ernest. *Casey at the Bat*. Paul Frame, illustrator. Englewood Cliffs, N.J.: Prentice-Hall, 1964.

Williams, Linda. *The Little Old Lady Who Was Not Afraid of Anything*. Megan Lloyd, illustrator. New York: Harper & Row/Trophy Books, 1986.

Yagawa, Sumiko. (Katherine Paterson, reteller.) *The Crane Wife*. Suekichi Akaba, illustrator. New York: William Morrow, 1981.

Song Picture Books

Aliki. *Go Tell Aunt Rhody*. New York: Macmillan, 1974. (Musical score included)

———. *Hush Little Baby*. Englewood Cliffs, N.J.: Prentice-Hall, 1968. (Score)

Chase, Richard. *Billy Boy*. Glen Rounds, illustrator. Chicago: Golden Gate, 1966. (Score)

Freschet, Bernice. *The Ants Go Marching*. S. Martin, illustrator. New York: Charles Scribner's Sons, 1973. (Score)

Hale, Sarah Joespha. *Mary Had a Little Lamb*. Tomie dePaola, illustrator. New York: Holiday House, 1984. (Score)

Hazen, B. *Frère Jacques*. Lilian Obligado, illustrator. New York: Lippincott, 1973. (Score in French and English)

Keats, Ezra Jack. *The Little Drummer Boy*. Words and music by K. Davis, H. Onorati, and H. Simeone. New York: Macmillan, 1968. (Score)

Langstaff, John. *Frog Went A-Courtin'*. Feodor Rojankovsky, illustrator. New York: Harcourt Brace Jovanich, 1972. (Score)

———. *Oh, A'Hunting We Will Go*. Nancy Winslow Parker, illustrator. New York: Atheneum, 1972. (Score)

Nic Leodhas, Sorche. *Always Room for One More*. Nonnie Hogrogian, illustrator. New York: Holt, Rinehart and Winston, 1965. (Score)

Rounds, Glen. *Casey Jones*. Chicago: Golden Gate, 1968. (Score)

———. *The Strawberry Roan*. Chicago: Golden Gate, 1970. (Score)

———. *Sweet Betsy from Pike*. Chicago: Children's Press, 1973. (Score)

Quakenbush, Robert. *Old MacDonald Had a Farm*. New York: Harper and Row, 1972. (Score)

Seeger, Pete, and Charles Seeger. *Foolish Frog*. New York: Macmillan, 1973. (Score)

Spier, Peter. *Fox Went Out on a Chilly Night*. New York: Doubleday, 1961. (Score)

———. *London Bridge Is Falling Down*. New York: Doubleday, 1964. (Score)

Wescott, Nadine. *The Old Lady Who Swallowed a Fly*. New York: Harcourt, 1980. (Score)

Zemach, Harve. *Mommy Buy Me a China Doll*. Margot Zemach, illustrator. New York: Farrar, Straus and Giroux, 1975. (No score).

Chapter 7: Storytelling and Drama

Aardema, Verna. *Princess Gorilla and a New Kind of Water: A Mpongwe Tale*. Victoria Chess, illustrator. New York: Dial, 1987.

———. *Who's in Rabbit's House?* Leo and Diane Dillon, illustrators. New York: Dial, 1977.

Alexander, Lloyd. *Taran Wanderer*. New York: Holt, Rinehart and Winston, 1967.

Baylor, Byrd. *Sometimes I Dance Mountains*. New York: Charles Scribner's Sons, 1973.

Bennett, Jill. *Teeny Tiny*. Tomie de Paola, illustrator. New York: G. P. Putnam's Sons, 1986.

Berger, Barbara. *Grandfather Twilight*. New York: Philomel, 1984.

Brenner, Barbara. *The Snow Parade*. Mary Tara O'Keefe, illustrator. New York: Crown, 1984.

Brown, Marcia. *Stone Soup*. New York: Charles Scribner's Sons, 1947.

Burningham, John. *Time to Get Out of the Bath, Shirley*. New York: Harper, 1978.

Byars, Betsy. *The Night Swimmers*. Troy Howell, illustrator. New York: Delacorte, 1980.

Cleary, Beverly. *Henry Huggins*. Louis Darling, illustrator. New York: William Morrow, 1950.

_____. *Ramona the Pest*. Louis Darling, illustrator. New York: William Morrow, 1971.

Clymer, Eleanor. *The Get-Away Car*. New York: E.P. Dutton, 1978.

de la Mare, Walter. *Molly Whuppie*. Errol Le Cain, illustrator. New York: Farrar, Strauss and Giroux, 1983.

de Paola, Tomie. *Fin M'Coul: The Giant of Knockmany Hill*. New York: Holiday House, 1981.

_____. *Pancakes for Breakfast*. New York: Harcourt, 1978.

_____. *Strega Nona*. Englewood Cliffs, N.J.: Prentice-Hall, 1975.

de Regniers, Beatrice Schenk. *Little Sister and the Month Brothers*. New York: Clarion, 1978.

Domanska, Janina. *What Happens Next?* New York: Greenwillow, 1983.

Ets, Marie Hall. *Gilberto and the Wind*. New York: Viking, 1963.

Fuchs, Erich. *Journey to the Moon*. New York: Delacorte, 1969.

Fritz, Jan. *Where Do You Think You're Going, Christopher Columbus?* Margot Tomes, illustrator. New York: G. P. Putnam's Sons, 1980.

Galdone, Paul. *The Little Red Hen*. New York: Seabury, 1973.

_____. *The Magic Porridge Pot*. New York: Clarion, 1976.

_____. *The Three Wishes*. New York: McGraw-Hill, 1961.

_____. *What's in Fox's Sack? An Old English Tale*. New York: Clarion, 1982.

George, Jean Craighead. *My Side of the Mountain*. New York: E. P. Dutton, 1959.

Ginsburg, Mirra. *How the Sun Was Brought Back to the Sky*. New York: Macmillan, 1975.

_____. *Mushroom in the Rain*. José Aruego and Ariane Dewey, illustrators. New York: Macmillan, 1974.

Goodall, John. *Midnight Adventures of Kelly, Doc and Esmeralda*. New York: Atheneum, 1972.

Grimm Brothers. (Anthea Bell, translator.) *The Brave Little Tailor*. Otto S. Svend, illustrator. New York: Larosse, 1979.

_____. (Elizabeth Shrub, translator.) *The Bremen Town Musicians*. Janina Domanska, illustrator. New York: Greenwillow, 1980.

Harding, Lee. *The Fallen Spaceman*. John and Ian Shoenherr, illustrators. New York: Harper, 1980.

Hastings, Selina. *Sir Gawain and the Loathly Lady*. Juan Wijngaard, illustrator. New York: Lothrop, 1985.

Hautzig, Esther. *A Gift for Mama*. Donna Diamond, illustrator. New York: Viking, 1981.

Hogrogian, Nonny. *One Fine Day*. New York: Macmillan, 1971.

Houston, James. *Black Diamonds: A Search for Arctic Treasure*. Toronto: McClelland and Stewart, 1982.

_____. *Frozen Fire: A Tale of Courage*. Toronto: McClelland and Stewart, 1977.

Hutchins, Pat. *The Doorbell Rang*. New York: Greenwillow, 1986.

_____. *Happy Birthday Sam*. New York: Viking, 1981.

Keats, Ezra Jack. *The Snowy Day*. New York: Viking, 1962.

Keller, Holly. *Geraldine's Blanket*. New York: Greenwillow, 1984.

Kimura, Yuriko. (Peggy Blakely, translator.) *Christmas Present for a Friend*. Nashville, TN: Abingdon Press, 1985.

Konigsburg, Elaine. *From the Mixed-Up Files of Mrs. Basil E. Frankweiler*. New York: Atheneum, 1967.

L'Engle, Madeline. *A Wrinkle in Time*. New York: Farrar, Strauss, 1962.

Little, Jean. *Mama's Going to Buy You a Mockingbird*. Toronto: Penguin, 1984.

Lobel, Anita. *The Straw Maid*. New York: Greenwillow, 1983.

Lobel, Arnold. *Ming Lo Moves the Mountain*. New York: Greenwillow, 1982.

McDermott, Gerald. *The Stonecutter: A Japanese Folktale*. New York: Viking, 1975.

McGovern, Ann. *Too Much Noise*. New York: Houghton Mifflin, 1967.

Merrill, Jean. *The Pushcart War*. New York: Addison Wesley, 1964.

Munsch, Robert. *Millicent and the Wind*. Suzanne Duranceau, illustrator. Toronto: Annick, 1984.

Paterson, Katherine. *Bridge to Terabithia*. Donna Diamond, illustrator. New York: Thomas Y. Crowell, 1977.

_____. *Come Sing, Jimmy Jo*. New York: E.P. Dutton, 1985.

Pomerantz, Charlotte. *Where's the Bear?* Byron Barton, illustrator. New York: Greenwillow, 1984.

_____, reteller. *Whiff, Sniff, Nibble and Chew: The Gingerbread Boy*. Monica Incisa, illustrator. New York: Greenwillow, 1984.

Pyle, Howard. *The Story of King Arthur and His Knights*. New York: Charles Scribner's Sons, 1983.

Shannon, George. *Dance Away*. José Aruego and Ariane Dewey, illustrators. New York: Greenwillow, 1982.

_____. *Piney Woods Peddler*. Nancy Tafuri, illustrator. New York: Greenwillow, 1981.

Slobodkin, Esphyr. *Caps for Sale*. New York: Addison Wesley, 1947.

Spier, Peter. *Dreams*. New York: Doubleday, 1986.

Turkel, Brinton. *Deep in the Forest*. New York: E. P. Dutton, 1985.

Van Allsburg, Chris. *The Mysteries of Harris Burdick*. New York: Houghton Mifflin, 1984.

Voight, Cynthia. *Dicey's Song*. New York: Atheneum, 1983.

Ward, Lynd. *The Silver Pony*. New York: Houghton Mifflin, 1973.

Waterton, Betty. *A Salmon for Simon*. Ann Blades, illustrator. Vancouver: Douglas and McIntyre, 1978.

Williams, Jay. *The Sword of King Arthur*. Louis Glanzman, illustrator. New York: Thomas Y. Crowell, 1968.

Wolkstein, Diane. *The Magic Wings: A Tale from China*. New York: E.P. Dutton, 1986.

Yolen, Jane. *Dinosaur Dances*. Bruce Degan, illustrator. New York: G.P. Putnam Sons, 1990.

Young, Ed. *The Other Bone*. New York: Harper and Row, 1983.

Zemach, Harve. *Duffy and the Devil*. Margot Zemach, illustrator. New York: Farrar, Straus, Giroux, 1973.

Zemach, Margot. *It Could Always Be Worse*. New York: Scholastic, 1979.